In the beginning

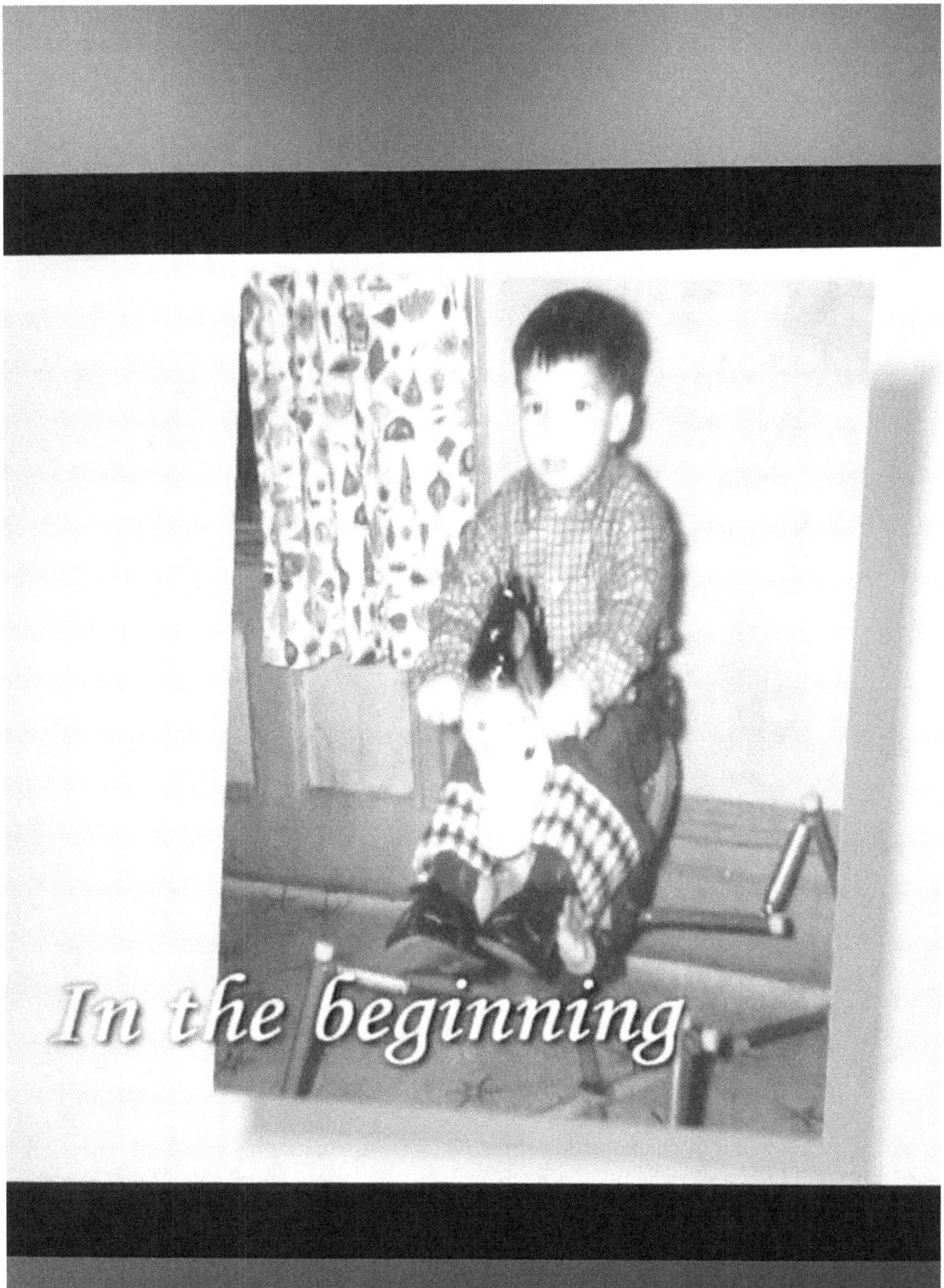

CHAPTER 1

In the beginning, this is the true story of Georgie Lozada aka. Jorge Lozada Jr. better known to others as Jorgito, and to others I am better known as Spanish Georgie from 110th Street in Spanish Harlem. In the penitentiary my other names are El Menor, El Abogado or Sing-Sing.

These are names that they gave me while doing time in different prisons.

Born June 21st, 1957. Bronx, New York. Lincoln Hospital. Across the street from the Yankee Stadium, that means I'm officially a Bronx Bomber.

My father and mother abandoned me when I was six months years old. They left me with a neighbor and as far as I know they abandoned me. The neighbor handed me over to my grandmother, Clara Vasquez. We then flew to Puerto Rico. I spent most of my childhood running the streets of San Juan. I went to live in La Perla, Puerto Rico with my grandmother, my aunt Matilda and my uncle Angel Lozada. The man with all the gallos de pelea (rooster fighters). I saw violence at an early age. People would shoot each other over rooster fights. From there, I went to live in Old San Juan la Calle de la Cruz.

Where Pedro Albizu Campos, a Puerto Rican attorney and politician the leading figure in the Puerto Rican independence movement had lived.
Many people in Puerto Rico consider Harvard educated Dr. Pedro Albizu Campos the father of the Puerto Rican Independence Movement.

I had lived in Old San Juan but my grandmother wanted to take me away from there because there were always fights, stabbings, shootings, prostitution and drugs were rampant. So my grandmother decided to move down to La Marina in front of the prison 'La Princessa'.

I recall as a young kid walking down to La Puerta de San Juan and getting cocolias (crabs) and go fishing or swimming. Those were beautiful times. I loved Puerto Rico. While living in front of the prison, I got very familiar with all the inmates that used to work outside the penitentiary. They knew me by name but they used to call me 'Jorgito'. I got an early start knowing the streets of Puerto Rico.

I must have been about seven years old when I saw prostitution, shootings, stabbings in Puerto Rico. I had gotten a college education at an early age on criminal justice and criminal law. I had seen it all already by six years old.

The only thing that I basically learned from my experience in Puerto Rico was that I got a B.A. in Criminal Law and Street Justice. My grandmother and I would travel back and forth from Puerto Rico to New York City, La Guardia Airport. It was a different lifestyle, the clothes, the style, the language & the way of living between both states. I loved Puerto Rico, but there was something about New York City that my grandmother liked. So she decided to make it official and go live in Spanish Harlem.

I met my little brothers for the first time in seven years. I was so excited that I was finally living in New York City in Spanish Harlem. It's not that I didn't like Puerto Rico, I loved it and still do to this day. But I'm a Yankee and a Yankee loves New York City. Everything was so fast paced in the city, outside of the law. I moved into an apartment with my grandmother on 1774 Lexington Avenue on 110th Street, better known as 'Across 110th Street'. This is where gangsters like Frank Lucas & Nicky Barns controlled the drug trade.

While living on 110th Street there were so many riots between The Black Panthers, The Young Lords, The N.Y.P.D., that I was experiencing a different lifestyle. Every other day they were shooting somebody downstairs. While I was attending school there were drug deals on every corner. At an early age, I aspired to be a drug dealer. Why? That's all I was used to seeing. Big lines, people copping dope and shooting up in my building on the roof. I never saw any of that shit in Puerto Rico. If they were shooting up, I didn't see them. But I was fully aware of what was happening in Spanish Harlem. So many things had corrupted my life, my mind and my soul.

I stopped going to school and started helping drug dealers by stashing their drugs in my house. I was getting a good education in true crimes of the drug world. So what do you know, I started selling joints outside of my building. At a dollar each I would sell about a hundred, but that's pretty good for a kid at eight years old. My father used to live next door to me with my other three brothers, and I would live with my grandmother in the next apartment. He would complain to my grandmother all the time about me selling weed, about me smoking it and my grandmother would respond by telling him "Until you start taking care of him and paying his bills and buying him clothes, don't say anything about him to me. You left him with a neighbor as a kid at six months."

My grandmother would let me run wild. I would hide guns in my apartment, bundles of heroin, drugs and virtually anything that the drug dealers would give me to stash. I started selling half ounces and ounces, nickel bags, dime bags of weed at the time. Everybody sold Heroin, but I sold weed. Heroin was a big thing in those days. I recall going to buy a couple of pounds of weed from a Colombian dealer that would have all the weed you could imagine. Pounds and pounds of it, he had it. He gave me about two grams and told me see if you could sell this in Harlem. So I took the cocaine and gave it to a guy named **Johnny Flores**. He would sell all of the Heroin in front of my building. He would become a father figure to me.

When I gave him the cocaine, we went into an apartment in my building and shot it up and said to me "Where can I get more of this coke from?" It was top shelf purity and he knew it. Thirty years ago coke was pure, but today it is pure garbage. So we bagged it up right away, and sold a few dimes in about ten minutes. The next thing I know he was asking for more.

Graduation time. From the weed to the coke, that's how I began my career. Going to Brooklyn back and forth, Johnny was schooling me as I went along. I went along on a journey of trouble, but I didn't know any better. I was just about fourteen or fifteen years old. But because my people in Spanish Harlem, that was popping in the 70's, and 80's, 90's. Now it's just getting worse. Everybody wants to be a drug dealer, a pimp, or a gangster. That's the knowledge I picked up from my teacher, Johnny Flores, my second father. He told me how to cut it, how to bag it, taste it without shooting it.

I wasn't a bad kid. Now looking back, I wasn't bad I just didn't have anyone to teach me, guide me or show me the love that I needed, besides criminology. I could have been the champ of the world, welterweight, if I had a father like Tito Trinidad's father Felix. I admire what he has done with his son throughout the years. I took boxing at an early age, and I really liked it. I was pretty good at it, I used to go to the famous Gleason Gym in Brooklyn under the Brooklyn Bridge. But I was more into rest, dress and do the best. I got involved with the cocaine business. I was making anywhere between 700 and 1,000 dollars per day.

I was attending Benjamin Franklin High School on 116th street Pleasant Avenue. Right down the block on 114th street was Rao's Italian restaurant founded in 1896. A gangster spot. I would sit across the street from the school and see them Lincoln's, Town Cars, Cadillacs and three-piece suits with gator snake shoes & lizards. True Italian Stallions. I wanted to look exactly like them, they were sharp dressers. But because I lived on 110th street in Spanish Harlem, I would go shopping to 125th street between 8th and 9th by Sylvia's Soul Food restaurant. I would go to eat there, collard greens and corn bread and barbecue chicken. That's where I first saw the real players of Black Harlem. The pimps, the realest gangsters up in that neighborhood. I was amazed how the black gangsters would control the whole streets of 7th and 8th avenue with Heroin. I guess I was still learning the game. I was being turned out without me even knowing I was being flipped.

It's easy in Spanish Harlem and Black Harlem to be at the age of 16 and seen everything and done everything. The true story of Georgie Lozada – Jorge Lozada.

As far as I recall, I began to sell cocaine to everybody and anybody that would pull up in a long limousine, talking about 'Where can I get some cocaine?' I would come down by 1 o'clock in the afternoon and I would work till 2 or 3 o'clock in the morning. There was so much action at 110th street Spanish Harlem or 'El Barrio' at early hours of the morning. People would be coming after hours looking for coke to keep going through the night to make it through the afternoon the next day. On 110th Street, there used to be an after hour club that would open up at 3 a.m. and everybody would hang out there from Hector Lavoe (the Singer), Hector Macho Camacho, Pete El Conde and a lot of people from the Baja Mundo (Underworld). That spot be running from 3 in the morning till 3 p.m., sometimes even longer. That's what an 'after hour' was back then.

The first time I ever got arrested, I was home sleeping just minding my business in Spanish Harlem. Some fool was calling me out the window, calling me out loud 'Georgie, Georgie, GEORGIE!!!'. So I looked out the window briefly then came down. As soon as I get into the streets, I am approached by my man Papo talking about "Yo I got these guys that want to sell a couple of guns they have." I responded, "I don't need no guns dude, I got the whole neighborhood with guns, they got my back." But anyways, I walked outside to the streets and walked inside another building on 111th street between 3rd and Lexington. The police roll up the wrong way and run into the building. Everyone spread but they caught me. Because they knew me. They've seen me, heard of me. But I always used to stay away from the police eyes, staying low-key.

So I got arrested, winded up on 100 Center Street, the court house in downtown Manhattan with a charge of possession of three guns. They blamed it on me. I went back and forth to court a couple of times and eventually dropped the charges.
The truth will set you free, John 8:32.

The Gift from God... The gift of God is eternal life through Jesus Chris our Lord – Romans 6:23

"Choose my instruction instead of silver, knowledge rather than choice gold, for wisdom is more precious than rubies, and nothing you desire can compare with her." Proverbs 8:10,11 - The Bible.

I wasn't always like this, so Christian. But after spending so much time in different penitentiaries, and doing some hard times from Las Tombas (The Tombs, Downtown Manhattan) to Rikers Island. You begin to grow up after many years behind bars, and your mind, your body takes a different look at it. At life behind bars.

In 1975, I had been selling cocaine for about two years. Most of my money would go to snake-shoes, suits, bottles, limo rides going to Coney Island and spending 500 dollars on Go-Karts rides. Taking a cab back to Spanish Harlem. I had no respect for money, but that's how it is each and every day of a drug dealer's life. Make it, spend it, and get some more. Watch your back from home invasions, from brother's trying to stick you up in the hallway, there's more to it than just being a drug dealer. For me it was a game, it was something I had learned through my childhood. I didn't know what I was getting myself into. If I knew what I know now, I would have never, ever, ever, EVER, sold drugs. I should have gone to college. I should have gotten a degree, a B.A., a P.H.D. I should've been an attorney, but no, I wanted to rest and dress, and do the best. I wanted to pimp up.

That's how I rolled, in 1974 – I was sixteen years old.

1974, I was going shopping to go to The Old Copa Cabana at 10 East 60th Street, a gangster speakeasy founded in 1930. This spot was visited by mobsters such as Charles "Lucky" Luciano, and the rest of the Murder INC. The actual owners, elusive as they were, were originally Albert Anastasia and Frank Costello. It eventually passed hands to Carlo Gambino, then Paulie Castellanos until the government finally forced the MOB out in 1986.

This is I at the Copa Cabana, rest, dress and doing my best.

Allow no fear in your life.

I didn't choose this life, this life chose me. What do you expect from a kid that was raised in Puerto Rico, in front of the prison system? A kid with no father, no mother, nobody teaching me anything right.

They word have I hid in mine heart, that I might not sin against thee. Psalm 119:11

Do all things without murmurings and disputings; That ye may be blameless and harmless, the sons of God, without rebuke, in the midst of a crooked and perverse nation, among whom ye shine as lights in the world. Philippians 2:14, 15

Don't blame me, blame society, my mother, my father – but don't blame me. I didn't choose this life, the life chose me. As a kid, I didn't know what was to come of my life.

Always be loyal to your friends. Enjoy them.
A true friend is always loyal, and a brother is born to help in time of need- Proverbs 17:17.

It is harder to win back the friendship of an offended brother than to capture a fortified city. His anger shuts you out like iron bars-Proverbs 18:19, TLB.

For the love of money is the root of all evil: which while some coveted after, they have erred from the faith, and pierced themselves through with many sorrows. 1 Timothy 6:10

In 1975, I was seventeen years old. I had met my mother for the first time.

The question I always wanted to ask my mom was 'Why, why did you run off and leave me and you went on and had two girls and a boy and I didn't see you for seventeen years?' You should have paid me child support for all those years that I was living without you, and had no food on my table. Left me with a neighbor.

I don't hate, I participate. Another chapter in my life, its been rough and hard for me. That's why I turned to the streets, to the pimp game, to the drug dealing.

CHAPTER 2

Stay hungry for the truth, a wise man is hungry for the truth while the mocker feeds on trash – Proverbs 15:14, TLB.

That same year, I flew out to Puerto Rico. I would fly every month and hang out at Condado Beach, Isla Verda, Old San Juan, Puerte Tierra and visit my family at AA 48 Santa Juanita, Bayamon. Mi titi Elsie Lozada Vasquez, I would jump off the airplane and run to her house to eat arroz con gandoules y lechon (rice and beans with pork).

My titi Elsie Lozada Vasquez.

She was my aunt, my friend and my mother. A very good cook, 100% Boricua.

I would also drive out to Vega Baja and see my other titi, Raquel Crespo. I would go there and the first thing we ate were traditional Puerto Rican dishes such as Panapenes con Bacalow (Catfish) with green bananas, avocado right off the tree and let me not forget the big pinapple mangos right off the tree. I would visit my cousin Lucy and all her brothers and cousins, years later when I went to the penitentiary to do time for **murder** she stood by me like a real trooper.

Titi Raquel in Vega Baja, Puerto Rico.

Lucy and my other cousins.

In **1975** that same year I recall flying back. I had been in Puerto Rico for two days, I usually stayed two days, three days or just even a day. When things got hot at the block, I'd be out in San Juan by the beach. I recall landing at Kennedy Airport and took a cab to my house at 110th Street, Spanish Harlem. As soon as I walked into my house, I saw my grandmother and she was angry. She said somebody had broken into the house. They had come in through the fire escape and ransacked the apartment. They took some jewelry, money I had stashed I don't remember how much, but right away I knew it was someone that knew me and my movements. It was somebody real close, and years later I found out who it was and I cut him a break. That same day I had to pull out my guns at people in the hallway in my building. Late at night, the building was becoming a shooting gallery. My grandmother would tell me to be careful, be careful but I wasn't listening. I would continue to sell my grams, half grams, whatever I could.

The next day, they came to stick me up in the hallway. I came down like an eagle and saw them like a predator, and I already knew what a stick-up boy looked like, act like and talked like. So I was prepared. I had a 25 automatic with nine bullets in it. It had to be like three-thirty in the morning and I was coming to serve somebody, but they were trying to serve me. So I pulled my 25 automatic out and I opened the window and I took the 25 out the window and started firing. You should have seen them boys running out the door, I even chased them around the corner throwing lead at their asses. That was the life in Spanish Harlem from 1969 through 1975.

Georgie at age 15 years old with Clara Vasquez, my grandmother that became my mother, my father my friend & my second eyes until she passed away in my arms one day from a heart attack. Titi Gloria on the left, took care of me like a son in good times and in bad times. When she passed away I was doing time in prison.

Photograph of the Young Lords Party, founded on July 26, 1969. The New York Chapter grew to become a regional center of the Young Lords, after gaining national prominence in leading protests against conditions faced by Puerto Ricans which led to the takeover of the First Spanish Methodist Church in East Harlem on December 28, 1969.

My hood, 110th Street and Lexington

You take the 6 train to get to my Hood.

Graffiti in the hood depicting Puerto Rican flag and the movement

Cuchifrito Frituras 116th Street, El Barrio, N.Y.C. I would go there as a kid, about two or three o'clock in the morning and get pasteles, arroz con gandoules, rellenos de papa and all that good Puerto Rican food.

On **Saturday, February 20th** approximately two-thirty in the morning Luis Pabon calls me to come down. I was upstairs in my apartment 8 at 1774 Lexington on East 110th Street. I came down, I saw him and he said that he had a customer that wanted 3 ½ grams of coke. I said "Okay" and ran upstairs, then came back down with about an ounce and a scale to serve him 3 ½ grams. There were two guys inside the hallway and Luis Pabon. As I bend down to put the drugs on the scale, someone hit me upside the head with a gun.

BAJA MUNDO

Underworld. I couldn't believe all the blood that was pouring out of my head. They really, really hurt me. They cracked me with a gun upside the head when I wasn't looking. They took control of my jewelry, the money in my pocket and the drugs. They roughed me up, put the pistol in my head, took the keys from my house and headed upstairs into my apartment. My grandmother was sleeping. They opened the door to my house, one guy had the gun to my head and the other told my grandmother to stay quiet and everything was going to be okay. They started ransacking my crib like animals. Instead of keeping it real, gangster for real, "Where are the drugs, where is the money" and go – not taking advantage of my grandmother, she was old and was about to have a heart attack. I gave them the money, the drugs and the rest of the jewelry I had in the room and they were gone. That's called a home invasion.

They were gone, I promised my grandmother that I would make them pay – with their life. I didn't go to the hospital, I told my grandmother to go back to sleep and she did. I cleaned my head up with alcohol and lay in my bed thinking about what had just happened to me. They could've killed me and my grandma; dope fiends are like that. No regrets. The next day everybody in Spanish Harlem knew I had been stuck up. The word was on the street, and the word travels pretty fast about how I was invaded. I hit the streets hard with a double barrel shotgun inside a shopping bag, and jumped into a cab and told the cab driver to go through all the drug houses. I would stop at every drug house in Spanish Harlem looking for them. But because I knew everybody in Spanish Harlem, all the big boys and little boys they told me information about the two guys that invaded me. They were ratted out, nothing new for the hood. I was told the next day exactly where they would be hanging out in front of a club on 110th Street, down the block at a certain time.

On **Sunday, February 22nd** approximately 6:30 in the afternoon I shot homeboy in the head. I ran up on him and his boy inside the club with a 25 automatic pistol and nine bullets. The neighborhood was on fire, conga playing, music playing and shots being fired. All I could hear were screams, people ducking, they didn't know where the bullets were coming from. I started walking up the block with the gun in my hand like a real hitman. I was so proud of myself. I jumped in the cab and went to the Bronx.

At 10 p.m. at night, I was on eyewitness news and they were looking for me, armed and dangerous. The biggest mistake I ever made in my life. At the time I wasn't thinking, I was young and stupid with big cojones (balls) and everything I've learned on street life, that's all I know. That's all I know. What would you do? What would you do if somebody came into your house, late at night, hit you with a gun upside your head, threatening your family's life and ransacked my apartment violating me. Talking about how he's gonna kill me. So I went looking for him, and I found him and took care of my part. I promised that to my grandmother. She was shocked, the whole neighborhood was stunned that a 17 year old boy would commit murder, gangster style, hitman style. They didn't call me crazy Georgie for nothing.

I arrive in the Bronx to my mother's house with my sisters and my step-father and by the time I got to the house they already heard the news on TV. They had my picture up on TV. That day the nightmare began, part two of my street life as a young boy facing time – facing 25 to life. Once in my life, I started thinking worried to death. They didn't know what to do, whether I should run to Puerto Rico and hideout or turn myself in. Everybody was telling me what to do and what not to do. I was so confused, I had been confused all my life but this time it was different. After discussing it with my family, with my tio Tono Martinez who was like a father to me, and good to me like a kid. He had whipped my ass a couple times but I trusted him, so what he said to me was that I was young and to turn myself in. That's exactly what I did.

I turned myself in to the East Harlem 23rd Precinct on East 102nd Street, New York City.

The 23rd Precinct serves East Harlem (El Barrio) north of East 102nd.

I turned myself in with two attorneys and my uncle, they were charging me with murder one in the first degree. I was facing twenty-five to life. I was handcuffed, read my rights, put me in a cell and an hour later I was on my way with three officers straight to 100 Center Street to the Courthouse. That same night I saw the judge; they sent me to Riker's Island with no bail.

Taking a bus ride to Riker's Island for Murder one. What a nightmare.

Welcome home. I spent almost a year there without bail.

I used to look out my window and listen to the planes heading down to La Guardia airport, and I would think about the times going to Puerto Rico visiting my family and spending time at the beach. I would be up at 2, 3 o'clock in the morning thinking about what's going to go on tomorrow.

On days that I had to go to court, they would wake me up at 2:30 in the morning. I would be put in a holding cell for hours until the bus got there at 8

a.m. They would load us on the bus and send us to the courthouse tombs on 100 Center street in Downtown Manhattan.

As you see they would strip us, again, and again, and again until we saw the judge. We would sit there from 9 a.m. to 2 o'clock p.m. then the bus would take us back to Riker's. This would go on for about a year for me, once or twice a month I would go to court. It was driving me insane. But because I was from the streets, raised with no father no mother this was okay for me.

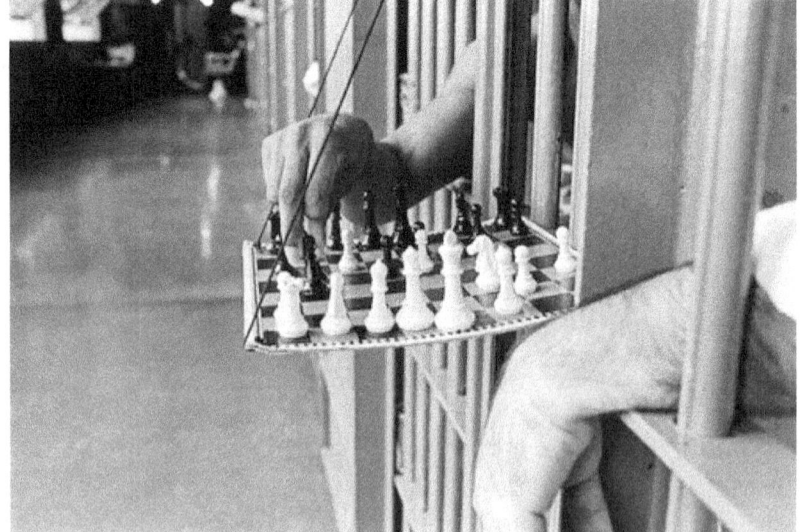

Many nights I would play Domino's, Chess or read low books. I would get them from the law library. I would read murder stories and cases related to mine.

You are on your own now. See, I didn't have that problem. I was from Spanish Harlem and 95% of the boys on Riker's Island are from Spanish Harlem.

Many nights I would spend seeking God asking for directions. I had just turned 18 years old. They transferred me from the Juvenile detention to 'The Block's' at Riker's Island with the older generation.

"A man is a fool to trust himself! But those who use God's wisdom are safe"- Proverbs 28:26, TLB.

"I will not leave you comfortless: I will come to you" John 14:18

"Lord, lead me as you promised me you would; otherwise my enemies will conquer me. Tell me clearly what to do, which way to turn"- Psalm 5:8, TLB.

Even gangsters cried out to the lord at night.

Serving time in prison is not supposed to be pleasant. I got right away involved with programs and getting my G.E.D. I started taking a course in legal research and started hanging out with all the law clerks. I started translating legal materials in English into Spanish and helping out the immigrants, Boricuas that couldn't read English.

Presos extranjeros piden ser deportados

ENRIQUE SORIA
EL DIARIO-LA PRENSA

Quince reclusos hispanos solicitaron al alcalde Edward Koch y al comisionado del Servicio de Inmigración y Naturalización, Alan Nelson, que se les deporte a sus países de origen por carecer de familiares en los EE.UU. Además, acusaron a las autoridades de deportar indiscriminadamente a presos indocumentados que quieren permanecer en este país.

El portavoz de los denunciantes, Oswaldo Rosero, dijo que los firmantes del pedido, confinados en Rikers Island, no han recibido aún respuesta pero tienen conocimiento de que algunos reclusos extranjeros en condición de ilegales han sido deportados contra su voluntad.

"Muchos de nuestros compañeros que tienen familia en EE.UU. piden ser juzgados en este país y rechazan la deportación", aclaró Rosero. "A los que quieren quedarse los deportan, y a nosotros que queremos irnos nos mantienen aquí".

Grupos que defienden los derechos de los indocumentados criticaron fuertemente hace semanas a varias personalidades políticas, entre ellas al alcalde Koch, por postular la expulsión del país de presos extranjeros que están a la espera de juicio y que se encuentran en condición de indocumentados. Koch presentó a fines de noviembre en Washington una propuesta para construir una cárcel en Brooklyn que albergue prisioneros extranjeros que van a ser deportados por traficar con drogas.

Por otro lado, dos vigilantes de este penal fueron demandados por el recluso George Lozada, que los acusó de hostilidad. Lozada, que funge como asesor legal de prisioneros en espera de juicio, dijo que su labor no cuenta con la simpatía de algunos vigilantes que lo hostilizan constantemente.

Además, dijo que se le había prohibido la entrada a la biblioteca del penal para impedirle realizar su labor de asesorar a los presos que no conocen sus derechos.

While at the law library I had taken a course in legal research on criminal law and passed it. I took the G.E.D. course and passed it. I would have never done this on the streets. I had plenty of time to study, day and night for a whole year. That's all I did, study, study, study and kept my nose clean. I helped a lot of 'presos extranjeros' with translation in legal materials. They were already calling me 'El Abogado'.

    While working at the law library for two dollars a day, I met a lot of inmate residents with drug cases, murder cases facing thousands and thousands of years. The more I read cases on some of the inmates, I couldn't believe how society was lost. I'm one of the 10,240 individuals doing time at Riker's. I became a bilingual law clerk, and for the first time in my life I was proud of myself. I always wanted to be a lawyer anyway.

    After a rough year going back and forth to court, going through the system at two in the morning spending hours in The Tombs holding cells waiting to see the judge. It was nightmarish. They stressed you out so much they made you plead guilty, without being guilty. It's a nightmare that I wouldn't wish on any young men. I finally got bailed out on a $150,000 dollar bail with the conditions that I wasn't supposed to go around Spanish Harlem.

CHAPTER 3

I am not proud of the mistake I made in my life that would probably cost me the rest of my life many, many years in the penitentiary. I am sure that you would have done the same thing as I did. I wasn't brought up with no silver spoon, I was from the hoods in Puerto Rico and in the hoods of New York City. I only did what I had learned on the streets.

But the individual that I shot, I come to know him years later that he did what he did as a hobby through years. Robbing the number guys in the neighborhood, sticking up bodegas, and doing home invasions. So he finally got what was coming to him. As soon as people found out in the neighborhood who I had shot, they were celebrating. They were terrified and scared of this individual, you couldn't walk the streets of Spanish Harlem with this guy and two other people sticking you up.

The big house for the big boys: Clinton Correctional Facility is classified as a maximum-security correctional facility for males 16 years of age and older and is the largest & third oldest facility in New York State, presently confining approximately 3,000 inmates. Most of them were all New Yorkers out of Spanish Harlem and in The Bronx. Most of them doing time for drugs, murder, kidnapping, the worst crimes.

I got released on bail with the help of family members, and the OG's from Spanish Harlem. A lot of them put thousands of dollars to come up with the one-fifty. I needed to get out on bail. So as soon as I got out of 100 Center Street, I ran up to Spanish Harlem. I started showing my face around the neighborhood, they were calling me 'Robin Hood' and telling me I had cojones. But they would have done the same thing too if somebody had invaded you with your grandmother and being pistol-whipped. What would you do?

Even the detectives that I turned myself into at 23 Precinct were talking about the individual I killed, how much of a scumbag he was and how he had it coming to him. I did them a favor by taking him out. The word was on the street that Georgie was back on the street. I wasn't worried about doing time, my family was behind me and Spanish Harlem was behind me. I was young and I didn't know any better. I didn't know what was coming to me.

I started going back and forth to court, fighting my case from the streets. I really didn't know what was going to happen to me, but I was ready. My attorney started going back and forth with plea deals or going to trial with this case. There was no way I had wanted to go to trial; I learned that a year later when I was working at the law library in Riker's. I read many criminal cases while I was working at the library, and from experience and other inmates there were certain cases you fight and there's some cases you suck it up and go do your time if you committed the crime. There's no way out, if you commit a crime you do the time.

Thank God it was over. I was tired of going back and forth to court. I finally took a plea deal of seven years. If I 'd gone to trial, I probably would have got 25 to life. But because of the situation of the case, the investigation in part of the detectives and a petition in Spanish Harlem from the bodegas, people in the neighborhood, going to court and supporting me and the long record of the individual that I killed made a difference in the plea deal that I took.

I had a clean record. The narcotics cops knew me I wasn't a trouble-making kid; I was out of their faces. I was never, ever in any trouble not even for loitering on the streets. I always respected the law.

John 8:32 'The truth will set you free'

"And you shall know the truth, and the truth shall make you free." John 8:32

"A wise man is hungry for truth, while the mocker feeds on trash"- Proverbs 15:14, TLB.

I went to court in **December 15, 1976** to turn myself in and take my plea deal of 0 to 7 years. I could do 5 or I could do the whole 7 depending on my behavior and what I accomplished while behind bars in a state penitentiary. The judge was nice enough that day, spoke to me from his heart, he said to me that he was going to sentence me to seven years and that he was going to recommend an early release. Depending on my behavior while incarcerated. He said to me that he was going to let me spend Christmas and New Year's with my family and that on January 1st I would turn myself over to the house of detention at downtown Manhattan.

Imagine if it was you. It's okay to shoot somebody, but then the consequences. I think to myself, I should've never done this dumb shit. Sooner or later somebody would have gotten, but the machismo kicks in and we become animals. We don't appreciate society and our freedom.

January came around pretty fast this year. I could not believe the reality setting in, in my life. I didn't know where I was going to go do time, I didn't know where I was going to be and sleep that night. But I sure as hell was going to find out. It was like a journey through a bad dream come true.

On **January 1st** at 9.am, on 100 Center Street in Manhattan, New York – I turned myself into the department of corrections. I was handcuffed; I said my goodbyes, see you later and the journey had just begun. What a nightmare. I was strip searched, butt-naked and put on a bus to Riker's Island.

My trip to Riker's Island was short and sweet. I was on the bus with murderers, rapists, traffickers, drug dealers, parole violators, with a bunch of wannabe gangbangers and mental problems. I spent a couple of days twenty-three hours in, and one hour out for recreation. I got all my food under the door like an animal. That's when reality sets in. It's 11 o'clock at night and all I see out of my little window is the sky. I hear the planes, but I can't see them. I'm in a cell all by myself. That's what happens when you don't use your brain and make mistakes. You need to focus in life. Take it for what it's worth, do you.

On the third day I was put on another bus and they drove all the way to Ossining, New York to Sing Sing Prison. Prison terminology "Up The River", "The Big House", and "The Last Mile" were coined there.

My new home, I didn't know how many days I was going to be there. I did my medical physical, I went through reception, met a counselor. I was fed food, put in a cell, given a blanket and a cot. I have done my homework on Sing Sing prison. That year, I was in Riker's Island prison I met a lot of murderers, a lot of killers and a bunch of gangsters that when I got to Sing Sing prison I had a lot of homeboys from Spanish Harlem – OG's. I recall my grandmother, titi Gloria, my cousin Tony Martinez and my little cousin Vanessa coming to see me for the first time at the prison.

I will always be grateful for my uncle, for bringing my grandmother to come see me. He was a good father, and a good uncle. Tough on me, but he loved me. While I was incarcerated I lost my aunt Gloria and family members. That's what happens when you do time in prison. Your loved ones, if you don't see them for years and years and they forget about you.

While in Sing Sing prison, I recall all the movies I used to see on TV about Sing Sing prison. I don't know if this was a dream come true, or something that I wanted in my life or had to go through in my life. I was in one of the roughest prisons in the world. I was in jail at the time with David Berkowitz aka 'The Son of Sam' who was a convicted American serial killer that began in the summer of 1976 killing six victims and wounding seven others by July 1977. I was transferred from Sing Sing to Elmira prison, about

12-13 hours from N.Y.C. I arrived there to the gladiator school of boxing at Elmira correctional facility.

I went right through the reception center, once again. Went through a program counselor that assigned me my program, which was a 3-year plumbing course. At the time I was taking a couple of college courses. I was also working at the law library. I wanted to keep my occupied, I wanted to stay as busy as possible, and come home as soon as possible. In 1976 when I arrived at Elmira prison, they had the Attica riots in 1975 and half of the population was from Attica. Serious criminals.

"The Hill"

Elmira Correctional facility is also known as the Hill and is a maximum-security state prison located in Chemung County, New York, in the City of Elmira. It is operated by the New York State Department of Corrections and Community Supervision. But I called it, 'The Gladiator School of Boxing'.

Most of the inmates that come out of Riker's Island and put up a front, acting crazy, once they get to Elmira Prison its a wrap. I started doing all the plumbing around the prison. I was taking a plumbing course at the same time. Every time someone got mad at the officers, they would plug the toilets with towels, toilet paper, whatever they could find – so that they could leave their cell for a while. I also started taking music and I picked up the trombone.

Here I am at Elmira Prison practicing my Trombone, in my hotel backyard.

I practice my trombone about two or three hours a day. Years later I begged to be in the jazz band with all the killers. They were professional jazz players from cross-country, doing time for different things. Some of them have been there ten years playing the bass, fifteen years playing the drums. The coolest cats I ever met in my life.

Years later, I started my own Latin band...

I used to run the Latin band in the music program.

You see me with my snake shoes and my trombone at Elmira Prison.

This is the local talent of criminals from the Bronx, Spanish Harlem, Lower east side, Brooklyn, Park Slope, and Jamaica Queens. Gang Bangers.

This was the Puerto Rican Discovery Day Festival. Yes I had good times, but I also had sad times when I missed my family and my freedom. There's nothing in the world that I would give up for my freedom.

I should have been the welterweight champ of the world. But I was caught up in the prison system, the prison life, street-life. I was confused. I did a lot of programs in the prison, plumbing, music, and cook in the kitchen, took college courses and worked at the law library. I didn't have time to be playing dominos, basketball, talking war stories or talking about what I'm going to do when I get out. I was going to do my time, stay busy and keep my nose clean. Hopefully I would get a transfer closer to New York City so that my grandmother could visit me. They used to drive hours to come out and see me.

My trainer named "Champ" a Muslim brother that had been down, many many, many years – 20 and change. Very slow spoken, respectful but very dangerous with his hands. - a very good professional trainer. Thanking you in advance for your time and concern Champ. - Respectfully, your student, Spanish Georgie.

CHAPTER 4: RELEASE DAY

After spending seven years in prison, I got out in **1982**. I got a job working for a plumbing company, as a plumber's apprentice. I was making good money at the time and I was attending John J. College of Criminal Justice. I was also working on the weekends for a real estate company named Frankie's Real Estate answering phones, attending to customers and office work. I was trying to get me real estate license. I started hanging out at the clubs, Copa Cabana, Roseland, Casa Blanca and going to all salsa concerts promoted by Ralph Mercado Production.

At the Copa Cabana in 1983.

That same year, I started thinking with my flesh again, my sinning ways. I was getting tired of working, breaking my ass up, studying all the courses at John J. College of Criminal Justice. I was swamped, and going out to the clubs: the Palladium on Monday nights, Tuesday nights Copa Cabana, Wednesday at Roseland back to Copa Cabana Thursday nights, Friday nights at Latin Quarters, Saturday nights at the Copa with Tito Nieves playing, finally Sunday nights at Studio 54. That's how it was each and every day of my life as soon as I got released from prison.

I started going to boxing matches at Madison Square Garden and I used to go to the famous Gleason gym, working out here and there. I didn't know what I wanted to do, be a boxer, a pimp, a lawyer, or be a real estate agent. I was confused smoking good weed, sniffing good coke, selling it – anybody would get confused. You soon start forgetting **prison**.

Trust the Lord completely; don't ever trust yourself – Proverbs 3:5, TLB

A man is a fool to trust himself! But those who use God's wisdom are safe – Proverbs 28:26, TLB

"As I sit here in this prison cell, I recall when things were going well, life has stopped for me. That's how it is each and every day of my life. It's up at 4 am, and do as I say" A quote from a Corrections Officer to Residents at the prison, when its time to get up in the morning.

We forget those days, when it's cold and damp in your cell on Christmas, New Years, Father's Day, Mother's Day, and your birthday.

The backslider in heart shall be filled with his own ways – Proverbs 14:14

I wanted to rest and dress, and do the best as always. I was in the street with all the players, ballers, shot callers, and wannabe gangsters. I started pimping, sipping, snoring and pimping backwards. I was on my way to the disaster. I was getting into the boxing game as well, training, managing and working at PAL Boxing teams.

North Bergen, New Jersey boxing team PAL. With Louie Lopez and professional cut-man Big George.

Georgie training with Hector Camacho in Las Vegas – Ceasars Palace.

Down in Long Beach, Mississippi with Macho & crew

Georgie with brother Victor, Hector Camacho and bodyguard.

Georgie with Tito Trinidad, father Felix Trinidad and Elio Rojas from Santo Domingo.

Jamie Fox at Madison Square Garden – Tito Trinidad vs. Mayorga

"My brother, can I manage you?"

Zab Judah vs Cory Spinks

At Camacho's fight at Ceasar's Palace, Las Vegas

At Condado Beach, Puerto Rico

Coked out of my mind, I forgot I had been in a penitentiary and I was playing Russian roulette again.

Yes, I was happy, I was pimping but just like anything it came crashing down.

Rest, Dress, and do the best.

    I wasn't trying to get serious with nobody. I started smoking cocaine in Miami. I took it to Puerto Rico, and back to New York. I wasn't really snorting anymore, we were freebasing at the time. I was smoking a half-ounce a day. That's all I did most of the time, stayed at the house and smoked my brains out. I feel sorry for myself, and every time I tried to stop smoking freebase I relapsed. It was all over the cities, all over Miami, Orlando, New York.

    At the time, I was pimping. I was three deep. I was working out of Midtown South, and I was living on Chelsea in New York City. I was doing well. I had all my girls on 25th and Park Avenue on the stroll. My main girl told me that she didn't want me selling any drugs at all. I was scared to death of it anyways. When I first came home, I couldn't get a job and I was smoking weed like crazy, snorting cocaine and smoking freebase. I was pimping backwards; I had forgot all that time I had done from Riker's through Sing Sing and up to Elmira Prison. That's what happens sometimes when you don't have a game plan and you forget about the times when you were incarcerated and mopping the floors in the gallery for a dollar a day.

"But every man is tempted, when he is drawn away of his own lust, and enticed. Then when lust hath conceived it, bringeth forth sin: and sin, when it is finished, bringeth forth death." James 1:14,15

I was taking chances late at night, running up town to Harlem, getting two-three or four 8 balls. I'll sit up at my spot with my ladies, drinking and smoking 'till the next day. That's how it was for months and months. I was getting money but I was smoking more than I was making. I was falling behind on my rent, I owed the dope man money and I was getting desperate because I just wanted to smoke. I wasn't smoking by myself, sometimes I had four bodies and we'd blow through half an ounce or an ounce in a couple of hours.

I was having hard times keeping my girls on the streets. They were getting arrested, going to court and spending money on attorneys. I was getting really desperate. The devil had me, I was a junkie and I didn't know it. And my girls were all junkies, but I didn't make them junkies because they came to me like that. They chose to be with me. They chose me.

I started having problems with other pimps over turfs. I started working on 37th and 8th Avenue, and every pimp in Mid-Town was trying to knock me for my hoes. They were blocking my money, they were making it hard for me to make money and they wouldn't let my girls work.

Pimp up. I started hitting the streets pimping, I was tricking the ladies on the street and I would charge them for asking me if I wanted a date. I would jump up and I would say real loud "Bitch, can't you recognize a pimp when you see one?" I'd be calling pimps at their hotels telling them their hoes wanted to be with me instead of them, knocking them. They chose me. I was creating problems in the pimp community, stirring up shit. I would get them fucked up on coke and smoked out; I put the pipe in their mouth and run off with them. I would be calling their daddy up and put them on the phone, tell them yourself you're with Spanish Georgie now.

I started flying to Puerto Rico and I started working Isla Verde where all the hotels were at in Condado Beach. I would go to El Caserio Barbosa and buy drugs but I was getting too hot in Puerto Rico with three ladies. So I shot back to New York to Times Square, had the girls working at 11th Avenue that's where I would charge the wrong prostitute. She turned out to be an F.B.I. Agent. I was stunned. She jumped on me like a cat; they were trying to charge me with robbery. I was stunned, shocked and handcuffed. I could not believe what was happening to me; not God, not attorneys or anybody could help me from this mess that I got myself in – once again in my life, for being stupid and ignorant.

I was charged with third degree robbery. The female F.B.I. agent was very nice with me, very professional. She started talking to me like I was a brother, like a friend. She started talking to me about God. At the time, I was down and dirty and I knew I was going to go do some time but I didn't know for how long, I had a record. But in a way, I was glad I was off the streets. I was confused, depressed and freebasing everyday – losing my mind. I was grateful to God.

I took a plea bargain of two ½ to five years. I didn't want to fight the case; I just wanted to get my life back on track again. That was a little taste of what it could be like. My family, my friends, my ladies and everybody I knew turned their back on me when I most needed them. They let me down, don't forget the prisoners but always once you get incarcerated – you're on your own. There's no such thing as family, friends just God 24/7 in your cell.

Six months later, from Riker's Island I was sent down to reception center at Downstate Correctional Facility and then to Collins Correctional Facility. There goes my journey again, here I go again.

CHAPTER 5

1987, I arrive at Collins Correctional Facility.

As soon as I got there, the place looked like a soft camp. But I knew about the spot when I had been doing time. I've done research on different prisons, when I was doing my last bit. I had knowledge that Collin's was violent.
It did have a good music program, a good bakery program and good overall educational program. But the violence there was just like Riker's Island, maybe even more dangerous because it wasn't a holding cell pen – you were doing time there.

The home of the birth of all the Latin Kings, los Hermanitos.

I got involved in the boxing program I started training again. My trainer was **Panama Lewis**. We hit it off right away; we started talking about Hector Camacho and other boxers. He started training Luis Felipe, a.k.a. King Blood and me.

During the early 80's, he was considered one of the best trainers of his time – compared with Emanuel Steward and Lou Duva. He was convicted of tampering with the gloves of Luis Resto in the Resto vs. Irish Billy Collins fight in 1983. With me, he was my friend and a good trainer. Yes there was controversy regarding the gloves, but I didn't think he needed to anything to those gloves. He was one of the best trainers in the world. We did 2 ½ years together and we were always laughing together.

Panama Lewis on the far left, and me on the far right.

I recall when Felipe talked to me and I was going home, he said to me "Don't come back, you're better than this shit."

I wasn't a Latin King, I was working at the law library once again and I was the president of the Latinos Unidos organization. I was running the music program.

Chico and Benny, amor del rey.

My clique, my friends, my brothers, mi hermanitos. I considered them mi familia.

With all the drug dealers, wannabe ballers, shot-callers.

While at Collin's Correctional Facility there were a lot of stabbings and extortion. A lot of marijuana and drugs being smuggled in, but most of the time I spent it at the law library. I was planning my release and I really wanted to focus this time on my life.

My Brother Edwin Lozada came to visit me at Collins Correctional Facility. He would always write me letters encouraging me, telling me how I had pimp bones in me and that he loved me. He used to correspond with me back and forth, come visit me on my birthday and drop money on my account. But one day I got a call from the dept. of security, they wanted to talk to me. When I got to the dept. of security's office, the Chaplin was there. I was informed that my brother had been killed on 112th street. He was shot in the back of the head. I was stunned and shocked, with all the respect I had in Spanish Harlem I couldn't believe someone had enough cojones to shoot my own brother in the back. The neighborhood knew they were going to have a problem because I had brothers, cousins, and payback time. I was informed by the dept. of security that they were going to take me to the funeral. They didn't want any problems out of me, and they asked me what officer would I feel comfortable with going on the ride. I said my dorm officer, he was a good officer and I felt comfortable with him. So we rode shotgun; two officers in the car, two in the back with shotguns with me and two in the front.

I was driven to Ortiz funeral in the Bronx with shackles. My whole family was looking at me shacked down when we arrived.

At the Ortiz funeral home in the Bronx and one of the saddest days of my life. He had paid me a visit just recently.

My father, my little brother Victor and I. My father was broken-hearted; he kept saying that he was going to get the guys that did it. I never saw him like that.

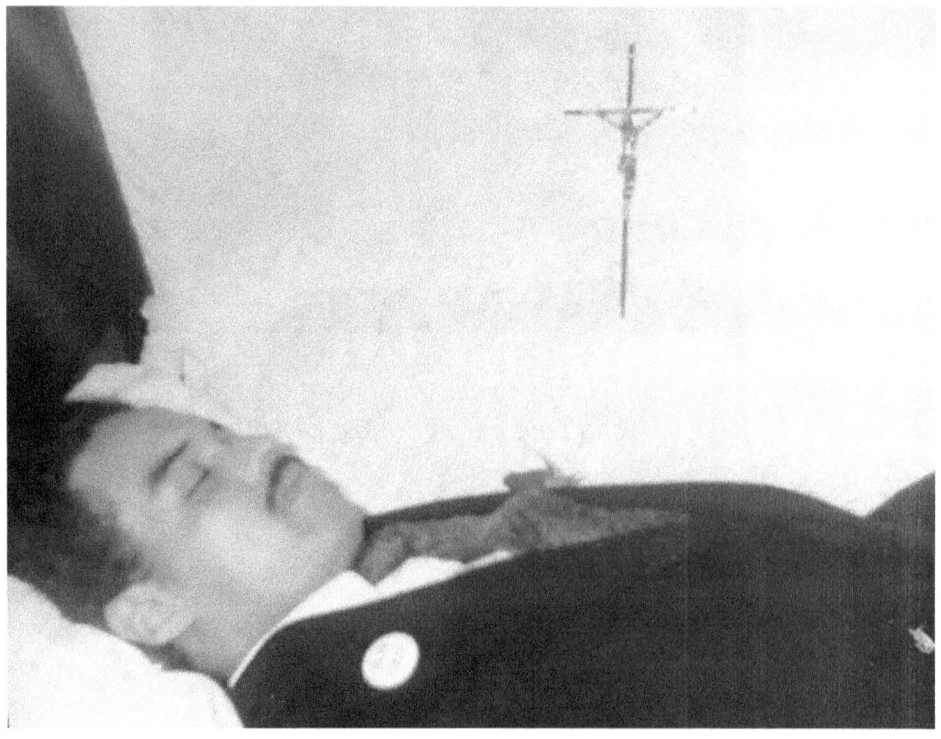

There must have been a thousand people there, they all came to see me and pay their respect. That's when I started really thinking about God...

"Do not repay anyone evil for evil. Be careful to do what is right in the eyes of everybody." Romans 12:17 (NIV)

The last letters from my brother, before he was shot down like an animal in the back. Cowards.

I was so angry, and I kept asking God… here's a kid who was accepted to Saint John's University, was going to be a fireman and worked at Bloomingdale Department Store on 59th street in the stock department. I couldn't understand why. God was treating me like this, but I didn't have an answer. I'm Christian, and I learned that the first time I was in prison up at Sing Sing for murder. The Lord looked out for me. Yes I got caught up in the street life, pimping, drugs etc. but I made a mistake again. I didn't want to get out losing a little brother like mine.

When I arrived back from the funeral, the first person that came to me was King Blood and Panama Lewis. I cried on their shoulders like a little boy. King Blood told me whatever I needed to let him know. I responded to him that it was a family matter, he knew who I was, he knew I had been at Sing Sing and worked at the law library. I was OG already and had done time in the penitentiary. I started going to church, reading the bible and praying. I was worried I was going to come home and shoot up the whole neighborhood. I was looking for guidance.

DEPRESSION & DISCOURAGEMENT

<u>I cried unto God with my voice, even unto God with my voice; and he gave ear unto me. Psalm 77:1</u>

<u>Have not I commanded thee? Be strong and of a good courage; be not afraid, neither be though dismayed: for the LORD thy God is with thee whitersoever thou goest. Joshua 1:9</u>

Me at Collin's Correctional Facility a year before I got released.

LOCAL

De regreso a

Un robo lo envió directamente a Sing-Sing, pero j

ENRIQUE SORIA
Segunda y última parte

Georgi Lozada le hizo un favor a su vecindario, aunque para hacerlo efectivo tuvo que recurrir al asesinato. Un despiadado criminal que tenía aterrorizado a El Barrio pagó con la vida el enfrentarse a Lozada, que lo mató de dos tiros en la cabeza. La justicia no lo perdonó y el vengador tuvo que desprenderse de su libertad por más de tres años, al salir de prisión tuvo que volver a empezar a vivir.

Georgi ya no era el mismo cuando salió de prisión y aunque la justicia —en cierta forma— fue indul-

el nivel de vida que tenía antes. A los 21 años, y con apenas seis meses de libertad, me compré un Oldsmobile"

frentarse a punta de pistola "chulo" de April, un afroa no macizo que ganaba co ramera mil dólares diarios.

"Ella no quería un ' quería un hombre que la a la protegiese. Yo fuí ese h me tenía bien y terminé en dome de un prostíbulo aun nunca supe nada de ese n antes. Cada prostituta cobra dólares la hora y nada que los clientes, que eran ejec abogados, porque cualer

---

guir dinero. "Quería hacer algo por ellas que siempre eran las que gastaban y me fui a Union Square y la calle 14, donde observé a una mujer con un collar de diamantes y lo puse en la mira. La seguí has-

GEORGI LOZADA muestra el pro y distribuye. De prisionero de las hombre de negocios.

'Mi experiencia como vendedor de drogas y el trato con las mujeres me sirvieron para bien. Un hombre de negocios me vio vender y me contrató para trabajar a comisión con un producto que recién salía al mercado...'

Georgi Lozada

I had a bout nine months before I got released. I started to practice my trombone more and more just to kill time. I spent time at the law library reading books. I didn't want to get caught up in anything so I kept my nose clean, I was tired of doing time and I was getting older. I spent almost 14 years of my life behind bars, I was <u>done</u>.

It was **1988.** Release day, my dad and my friend came to pick me up. I was proud of my dad that he was coming to get his son for once in his life. I know he was hurt because I lost my baby brother – and he didn't want to lose me. That's all he talked about on the ride back home to Spanish Harlem. A new beginning. The guy that killed my brother, I didn't have to go looking for him. He went to Washington D.C. and killed someone else during a robbery, he was sentenced about a 1,000 years – life imprisonment.

The first thing I did, I got on the phone and started making calls. I wanted to start my life all over again and have a new beginning.

"Choose my instruction instead of silver, knowledge rather than choice gold, for wisdom is more precious than rubies, and nothing you desire can compare with her."
Proverbs 8:10,11 (NIV)

For two days straight I spent it in my house. I had Hector Camacho pull up in front of my house in a convertible black Porsche. I looked out the window and the champ said "Come down" and he took me shopping that day. True story.

I was trying to consult this homeboy after he lost to Camacho

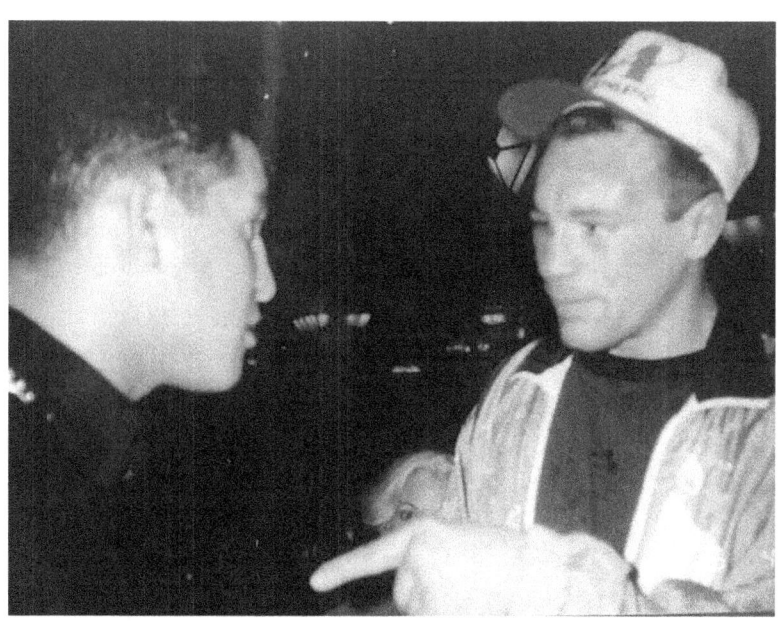

Camacho and the homeboy he ass-whooped.

I started going to all the fights with Hector Camacho, his wife Amy, and bodyguard Rudy his lawyer and manager Ismael Leandry.

Eating good at Ceasar's Palace. I'm grateful to God I'm released.

Me at the hotel.

It feels good to be out, I ain't going back inside. The Bossman, no drug dealer - CEO

Press Conference in 1989.

At the press conference – 'No pictures please!

CHAPTER 6

De regreso
Un robo lo envió directamente a Sing-Sing

From the Negative to the Positive

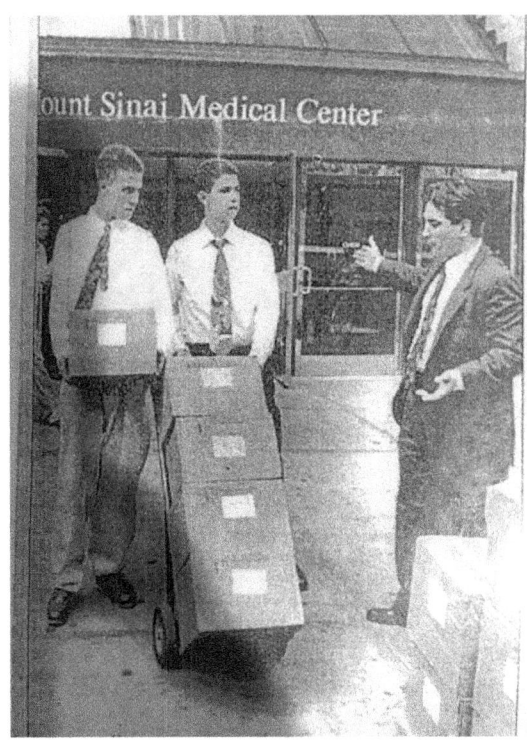

CON DOS DE SUS EMPLEADOS, Lorenzo Antenucci y Luis Félix, Lozada descarga su mercancía en el Mount Sinai Medical Center. La etapa de drogas y prisión quedó atrás.

Foto: OSVALDO PEREZ

Foto: OSVALDO PEREZ

GEORGI LOZADA muestra el producto que, ahora, él mismo fabrica y distribuye. De prisionero de las drogas se convirtió en un próspero hombre de negocios.

I started manufacturing and distributing an industrial, marine & aircraft-cleaning product for use in offices, medical, hotel, and restaurants in **1990**. It's an environmentally safe and 100% biodegradable product.

```
                    MATERIAL SAFETY DATA SHEET
                     SIMILAR TO OSHA FORM 20
------------------------------------------------------------------
                            SECTION I
------------------------------------------------------------------
MANUFACTURE/DISTRIBUTOR: Wonder Products
EMERGENCY TELEPHONE NUMBER: 1800-255-3924
 CHEMICAL NAME AND SYNONYMS: N/A PROPRIETARY BLEND
 TRADE NAME AND SYNONYMS: Wonder All-Purpose cleaner
 CHEMICAL FAMILY: Alkalin Detergent
 FORMULA: N/A BLENDED PRODUCT
 HEALTH-1     FLAMMABILITY-0     REACTIVITY-1     PROTECTIVE EQUIPTMENT-B
------------------------------------------------------------------
   SECTION II, HAZARDOUS INGREDIENTS
------------------------------------------------------------------
                                       CAS#              %           TLV UNITS
Water                                  7732-18-5        <5           None
Dipropylene glycol monomethyl ether    034590-94-8     <5           100ppmTWA
Polyethylene Mono (Nonylphenyl) Ether glycols  9016-45-9   >5       Not est.

   SECTION III, PHYSICAL DATA
```

El Presidente – CEO of Wonder Product

I was done selling drugs; I didn't have to pimp anymore. I was selling cleaning products from hotel to motel to the holiday inn. I was going mostly every weekend to different fights; I would always bring samples with me. I have been selling cleaning products for a couple of years now, and thinking of going into real estate.

When you are incarcerated, and you find yourself in cold, damp, cell on G-block or C-Block and on the lock-in for twenty-three hours a day and one hour out. For some reason you start using your brain and you turn to God. The lord has blessed me in mysterious ways, I'm grateful and I'll always be grateful to God first.

O my soul, why be so gloomy and discouraged? Trust in God! I shall again praise him for his wondrous help; he will make me smile again, for he is my God!" – Psalm 43:5, TLB.

BAD HABITS

I was born Catholic and Christian, I should have known better but I was young and stupid with no parents, no guidance. From La Perla in Puerto Rico to Old San Juan and then I lived in front of the prison La Princessa in La Marina. So I got schooled in Puerto Rico, I got a degree in criminology as a young boy. I picked up a lot of *bad habits* from La Calle (the streets). By the time I stepped into Spanish Harlem, I was playing my trombone out the window at 110th Street. Spanish Harlem was like the University of Princeton, Harvard, Yale, NYU, Hunter College, John J College of Criminal Justice (which I attended years later) of criminology.

I'm not proud, I am not proud of the bad habits I picked up as a boy over the years. But, today I am a C.E.O. of my own manufacturing and distributing company. Yes, I pay my taxes and yes I have an accountant. My experience, my knowledge of street life – '*street life, cause the only thing I know, street life*' has taught me to love God, to respect others, to be humble and happy and work hard to be successful. I am a true testimony. Anybody can come up, you ain't gotta sell crack, weed, heroin, crystal meth, imitation Rolex or coach bags. You want to be a drug seller? Work for a big manufacturer in the pharmaceutical industry – go door to door and sell it to the doctors legit.

You ain't got to be negative my brothers and sisters. Pimping ain't easy.

"The acts of the sinful nature are obvious: sexual immorality, impurity and debauchery; idolatry and witchcraft; hatred, discord, jealousy, fits of rage, selfish ambition, dissensions, factions and envy; drunkenness, orgies and the like. I warn you, as I did before, that those who live like this will not inherit the Kingdom of God." Galatians 5:19-21 (NIV)

"Work hard and become a leader; be lazy and never succeed" – Proverbs 12:24, TLB

Again, I am sharing my life testimony. I spent 23 hours in a cell and one hour out for recreation. At times hungry, confused but God been good to me – all the time. Yes I went through tribulations, but I would have never been me, the person I am today. This is for you when you get out on parole after spending, 10-15 years in prison. Do right my brothers, my sisters – do the right thing:

"The lazy man won't go out and work. There might be a lion outside! He says. He sticks to his bed like a door to its hinges! He is too tired even to lift his food from his dish to his mouth! Yet in his own opinion he is smarter than seven wise men" Proverbs 26:13-16, TLB

I ain't trying to preach to you brother, but that cell is no joke. I spent fourteen years in prison, doing a parole violation up in Sing Sing. I spent fourteen years out of my life like a dumbass New York Rican from Spanish Harlem, trying to be a shot caller and all I did was end up in prison, every time.

It's time to have fun and enjoy my life, and do the right thing. Giving all praise to God.

SHOWTIME

At Madison Square Garden, me and ICE-T – pimping ain't easy

1994 – 1997

Don't make no mistake, been there done that. God been good to me.

At Bonano Productions, straight up gangsters – BAJA MUNDO – UNDERWORLD. No te equivoques, me escuelita fue Puerto Rico.

You see me in the 90's

*Como los puse a gosar a todos, el Mercedes Benz stretch y dicen que soy loco
Pero Ismael Leandry dice lo contrario. El Zorro.*

Despues de la pelea, todos se fueron a dormir y yo me fui con el chauffer a buscar putas... God forgive me, pero fue la verdad. If you don't believe me, fly out to Puerto Rico to Isla Verde at J.C. Towers and ask Ismael Leandry.

Everybody else went to sleep again, and I went to pimp up

Not for nothing, but God been good to me after all that time I did in the penitentiary.

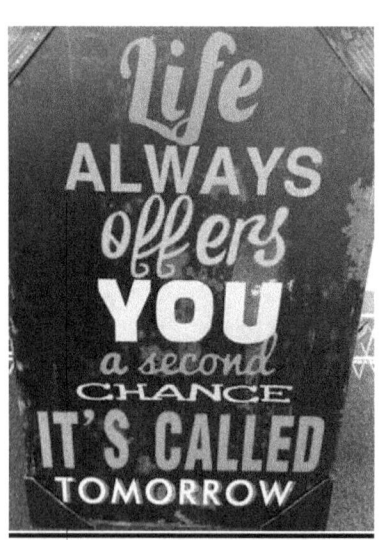

In Las Vegas with el famoso Ismael Leandry, Hector Camacho's manager.

I'm going to take out time from my busy schedule of writing my autobiography to say to the world and Puerto Rico, boricuas and New York Ricans from Spanish Harlem this is Camacho Team. We were faithful, regardless of what happened – we were there for Macho Camacho. But the Camacho team has always kept me in first-class with them, and they never elbowed me. Mad love to Amy Camacho, thank you for everything when I was incarcerated when I came home and you put me on. Thank you Amy. And to my main man Ismael Leandry, and your son Leandry Jr. el Abogado criminal de Puerto Rico and author of many, many books. Thank you for your love. Aqui estoy, presente.

Presente. Preguntale a Ismael Leandry faithful. Gracias Ismael por todo, when I was down and when I was up you didn't care you always gave me consejos (advice) – you always treated me like a son. When other promoters and everyone was around from Spanish Harlem we used to run a hundred deep. I always got a plane ticket from you, round-trip. Gracias, for telling me to stop doing drugs and not giving up on me. Especially when they killed Camacho, you opened up the doors of your mansion to me – thank you.

ISMAEL LEANDRY. TE QUIERO MUCHO – JORGE LOZADA, EL GEORGIE

To my Homeboy from Spanish Harlem, ay fuego en la 23 de la 110 st.... Thank you Raymond Mohammed for the plane tickets. For the wine & dine. Through the years you will always be in my heart for being faithful to me. Thank you. You're a true gangster, with all respect.

Pimping in Vegas before you were there, newjack.

Amy Camacho, thank you for looking out for me when I got out of the penitientiary. I'll always be grateful to you.

This is one of the best fights I ever attended. I was kicked out of the fight and then was let back in by the big boys.

Camacho and me at the press conference in Texas for the 'Opposites Attack' fight.

Camacho on the left and De la Hoya on the right at the press conference

For the big payday, 5 million plus that was pimping back then. That was serious money

Before the fight...

During the fight

ISMAEL LEANDRY – MANAGER

Rumble in Las Vegas - 1997

I remember that day; it was history in the making but all I was thinking about was the after party. Camacho Jr. and me were sitting together and watching the fight. As we watched the fight we got angry when De La Hoya was beating him up, but Camacho will always win or lose would come on top. He was a star, and today he's in the hall of fame. It's been a pleasure riding with you, R.I.P.

1997, Tribute to Orlando Merced

I will always be grateful to Orlando Merced, tu mama (your mother) was like a mother to me that I never had. Your brother Jose, put me on the map with El Paraiso disotech and you paid some of my bills that I owed when I was down and dirty. Your family was good to me, God bless you. – Spanish Georgie aka George Lozada

I should have listened to you Orlandito, I'm sorry. I went to the Camacho fight, and relapsed at the fight. I flew to Puerto Rico and really flipped out there. I was going down to Caserio Jose Celso Barbosa, Bayamon to cop and smoke crack. I ran out of Puerto Rico and ended up in Orlando, Florida. There I kept smoking crack and I couldn't stop. One night, I broke into a church and I cried out to God that I didn't want to smoke crack anymore, to please help me. I just wanted to break the church up; I was blaming God. I told God that if he didn't help me stop, that I was going to break into every church I knew in Florida and steal the equipment to sell it on the street.

I didn't need the money, I was mad at God. All I did was get myself jammed up for stolen property and because of my criminal record; I decided to make a plea deal. I was strung-out and just wanted to lay down my end. I just wanted it all to end, this addiction to freebase crack smoking. So I did 24 months and got into a drug program and a Christian fellowship. I came home from the State of Florida correctional facility – everybody knew me from the Cubans to the Boricuas, New York Ricans stuck in the department of corrections doing time. They go on vacation, and they come back on probation. People got it twisted with Orlando, Florida – they give you hard time there for stolen property. Another chapter in my life to get me in the right track again.

I cleaned myself up and went forward again. While I was there, I met Chaplin McGahey at Orange County Prison Ministry. He treated me like a father, a father I never had. I spent hours talking to him, telling him a whole documentary about my life – about how I didn't have a father or mother and I ran the streets of Puerto Rico and the five boroughs of New York City, especially Harlem. How I sold drugs, pimped girls never turned them out; they were always prostitutes and me living the street life. He said that God loves me and that he loved me and that as soon as I was ready to get out he would be there for me. Everything else is history. His family is my family today; I have gringoes in my family now.

Coming home, I got myself a job in Orlando doing concrete work – working at Disney grounds to save money and starting up my business again 'Wonder Products' and everything else is history. I'm back on track again. This time, I've got God.

"You could be Armed and Dangerous! Armed... with the Word of God, the best weapon to confront the forces of Satan at work in our world."

2000 - 2001

PRISON FELLOWSHIP Ministries

In recognition of participation in the seminar,

CHRISTIAN BASICS

GEORGE LOZADA

a child of God, is hereby awarded this

Certificate of Participation

"Be strong in the Lord and in his great power. Wear the full armor of God. Wear God's armor so that you can fight against the devil's evil tricks."
Ephesians 6:10–11 New Century Version

Charles W. Colson

Instructor

PRISON FELLOWSHIP
Ministries

In recognition of participation in the seminar,

GROWING IN CHRIST

GEORGE LOZADA

a child of God, is hereby awarded this

Certificate of Participation

"Be strong in the Lord and in his great power. Wear the full armor of God. Wear God's armor so that you can fight against the devil's evil tricks."
Ephesians 6:10–11 New Century Version

_____ _____
Charles W. Colson   Instructor

_____ 3·18·00
Chaplain   Date

In recognition of participation in the seminar,

"YOU ARE SOMEBODY"

Jorge Lozada

a child of God, is hereby awarded this

Certificate of Participation

on this **24TH** day of **JUNE**, 20**00**.

"Be Strong in the Lord and in his great power. Wear the full armor of God. Wear God's armor so that you can fight the devil's evil tricks."

Ephesians 6:10-11 New Century Version

Charles W. Colson   Instructor

Chaplain   Date 6/24/00

CHAPTER 7

Years later, in **2001** I bought my first house in New Jersey. I was working at the PAL Boxing Club in North Bergen, New Jersey.

This is my first house.

I rented out the first floor & second floor apartments and I moved into the basement apartment, and I kept the two-car garage for my business. At least it was bigger than a prison cell. I would park my first Mercedes AMG outside my two-car garage.

I would work hard until I made a hundred cases of Wonder Product, my all-purpose cleaner. I would distribute them the next day from Brooklyn to Long Island. To the homes point market and restaurants, car dealers. I started using the positive to beat the negative. I started thinking I'm a CEO, why sell drugs when I can sell cleaning products and work on re-orders.

I didn't forget about God, and I would never forget about God. I am armed and dangerous with the word of God. I'm no preacher and I don't really know the bible, I don't recall scriptures but I'll never forget my testimony. From the day I went to prison and the day I got out and went back.

"But without faith it is impossible to please him: for he that cometh to God must believe that he is, and that he is a rewarder of the that diligently seek him." Hebrews 11:6

"Therefore being justified by faith, we have peace with God through our Lord Jesus Christ." Romans 5:1

"...I tell you the truth, if you have faith as small as a mustard seed, you can say to this mountain, 'Move from here to there' and it will move. Nothing will be impossible for you...." Matthew 17:20 (NIV)

I started going to different churches, sometimes from New Jersey I would drive to Brooklyn to go to the Brooklyn Tabernacle. I then started going to Trenton, the hood at 400 Hamilton, New Hope Church. We would go from door to door and to the parks and invite people from the streets that needed God to come to church. Sometimes you got to give back. I promised God and myself that I would never forget the prisoners.

"I was naked and you clothed me; I was sick and you visited me; I was in prison and you came to me." Matthew 25:36

2002, *I got engaged to my wife Mariela and gave her a rock. She said "Yes".*

My sister-in-law Macielle, my nephew Eton Lozada, my baby brother Victor Lozada and my soon to be wife & me.

From **2001** to **2002**, once I got engaged to my wife I said to myself I needed to make money for the wedding, I needed to work hard. I had met an angel, a blessing from the sky & from the lord.

Miracle

I wasn't always a lucky guy with the ladies, most of the time I wouldn't meet a good girl. I always met a titty dancer, an escort girl, a drug addict, a wannabe – but one day I was introduced to my current wife by my brother. She was the godmother to my nephew; she was educated with a college degree. I had the gift of hustling and she had the education. She had a degree in accounting, that's how my business took off. The Lord was answering my prayers, this was a true miracle in my life and life was getting good after all that time in prison.

> *"Seek the LORD, and his strength: seek his face evermore. Remember his marvelous works that he hath done; his wonders and the judgments of his mouth…." Psalm 105:4,5*

"But my God shall supply all your need according to his riches in glory by Christ Jesus" Philippians 4:19

"Wealth gotten by vanity shall be diminished: but he that gathereth by labour shall increase." Proverbs 13:11

See, I wasn't always like this. When I was incarcerated, I was in the flesh. The more time I did and the more time I spent in those cells with 23 hours in and 1 hour out, the more I started to read the bible and pray. I started noticing that when I would pray out loud to God, I would see change. I don't know if you want to call it 'miracles' but I wasn't smoking any weed or crack when I saw them. My testimony will speak for itself and my criminal record as well. I am grateful to God.

Ambition

I started doing the boat shows & car shows at Javitz center for my business. I did restaurants De La Rosa on Broadway on 176, Casa de Mofongo, Medina's Bakery, Extreme Machines, Antonio's Restaurant one fine Italian restaurant in New Jersey, Hunt's Point Market, Elia's Car Dealer and so on. I was trying to save money for my wedding.

The banner I do Miami boat shows, Ft. Lauderdale, Javit's Center car shows in New York City.

In my office, keeping track of my customers with my 27" Apple iMac. You don't have one of these in prison, that's why I choose to stay on the streets.

I started worshipping at night, praying, asking for forgiveness and speaking from my heart to God. Please forgive me for whatever I have done out of ignorance God, and please forgive me for my sins Lord. Give me strength to keep going, keeping away from drugs, people, places and things. I am done Lord.

> "O come, let us worship and bow down: let us kneel before the LORD our maker." Psalm 95:6

> "Let all bitterness, and wrath, and anger, and clamour, and evil speaking, be put away from you, with all malice: and be ye kind to one another, tenderhearted, forgiving one another, even as God for Christ's sake hath forgiven you." Ephesians 4:31,32

I wasn't a hypocrite, I was just telling the truth John 8:32 'The Truth will set you free". I did the time, I spent time in prison in some cold damp cells for years with nobody, except me, myself, and God. I'm going to be loyal to him, because I've seen the miracles in my life with him. I don't like the flesh.

I would wake up every day; I first started with a hand-truck from door to door. I recall days when I would walk down Richmond Hill for hours and hours until I got my business. The Lord's been good to me, but I've been doing the walk and not the talk. Don't hate, just participate.

Wedding Day

2002

"The best and most beautiful things in the world cannot be seen or even touched. They must be felt with the heart." – Helen Keller

"A friend is the one who comes in when the whole world has gone out."

"Without true friends the world is but a wilderness." - Bacon

"God evidently does not intend us all to be rich or powerful or great, but he does intend us all to be friends." - Ralph Waldo Emerson

"Friendship has no name but love." - Habib Sahabib

Free at last, no more Riker's Island for me, no more Sing-Sing for me.

Con la familia (the family).

I'm all the way up, can't stop me now!

To my family, my wife's family, my brother Victor (I might be mad at you sometimes) I'm grateful to you to introducing me to my wife. To my family, gracias de Corazon, I will always be grateful.

You can't celebrate like this in prison.

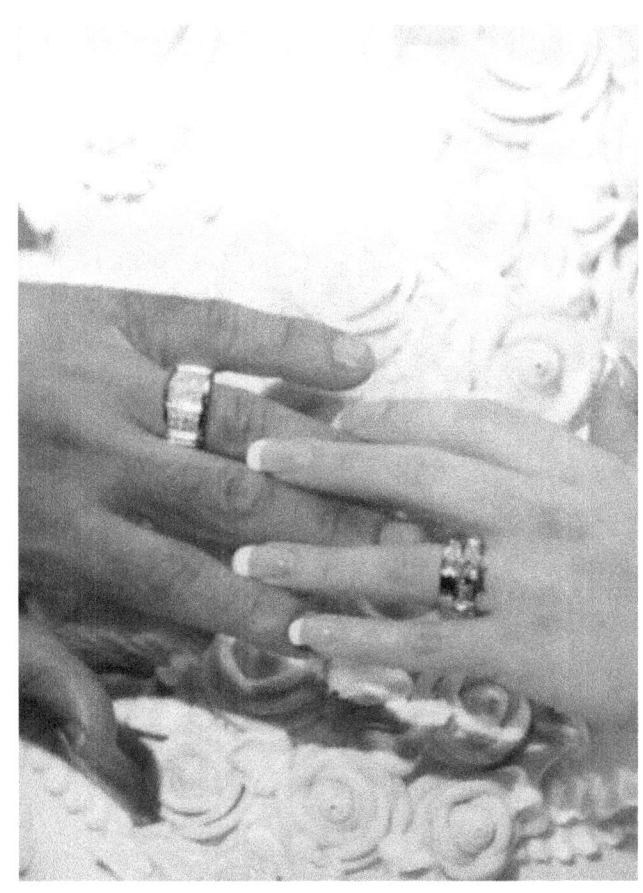

If you work hard, the Lord will bless you.

Honey Moon - 2002

2002 was an exciting year, I had just gotten married and took a flight to Puerto Rico with my wife and visited my grandmother's gravesite at To Alta. I went to Santa Juanita, Bayamon to visit titi Elsie and the rest of my family.

I wanted to walk through Old San Juan, La Perla, La Marina, and La Princessa (The Prison).

I was out of prison, and I was in Old San Juan my old stomping grounds, my college, and my university. Where my mother and family members were buried. I recall that day and I cried a lot, it was my honeymoon and one of the best times of my life but the memories haunted me.

Banco Popular brings me a lot of memories, my grandmother used to go to 116th street in Spanish Harlem to deposit her checks.

Puerto Rican plates.

After spending time in San Juan, dancing Salsa with my wife and walking through Old San Juan, crying and recalling my childhood I decided to go to El Conquistador a resort in Fajardo, PR.

Aerial view of Fajardo resort area

This morning I got up and said let me go for a run in Fajardo, and let me praise God for being so good to me.

"Blessed is the man who finds wisdom, the man who gains understanding... She is a tree of life to those who embrace her; those who lay hold of her will be blessed" – Proverbs 3:13,18, NIV.

To my wife...

"When you make new friends, don't forget the old. One is silver, the other gold." – Erasmus

I love you honey.

From the Riker's Island showers to the beach of Conquistador, what a good life.

Time to go back home soon

Thank you Puerto Rico for my vacation, and my education.

CHAPTER 8
2003

I got involved with PAL Boxing; I started working with young guys from the streets hoping to use my street knowledge to push them in the right direction. Sometimes it worked, sometimes it wouldn't but what would God do? The Lord didn't abandon me.

My brother peewee, head trainer at the PAL in North Bergen, New Jersey R.I.P.

With Mr. Mexico

Fighting at Mohegan Sun with Luis Lopez out of Jersey City, Ringside Boxing Club.

From the left: Luis Lopez, Mr. Mitt, Mike Tyson, Me and Mario (Owner of Ringside Restaurant & Boxing Club).

After a successful win with Elio Rojas Dominicano, pura sepa.

John Ruiz, Elio Rojas, & Jorge Lozada

Babyface, me and promoter. Old school.

Make no mistake, it's 'The Real Deal' aka 'The Warrior' Mr. Evander Holyfield, The Champ.

Zab Judah's belts

Some are boxers, others are champs. A true champ has a couple of belts.

From left: Brother, Father Yoel (his secret weapon), me and Super Judah. If I had a father like Yoel or Felix Trinidad, I would have been a champ – no questions asked. I ended up 14 years in prison, with Panama Lewis assault in the ring. Zab, thank you for your love. You never judged me and whenever you saw me you gave me love. When you fought Miguel Cotto, I was sad just like when Camacho fought with De La Hoya, I cried like a little baby with camachito jr.

Tuesday September 14th, 2004 approximately at 12 midnight, Jason Quick did his job. Here I am with the champ

Emanual 'Manny' Steward and Thomas Hearn's Jr. with me

Thomas Hearn's Senior with me on the same day.

For years, Don always showed me love and Super Judah and his brother Joelle and Mother, whole family always showed me love when I went to Zab's fights.

Super Judah and bodyguard at Madison Square Garden.

Fat Joe with me at the fight. I'm ALL THE WAY UP, nothing can stop me, I'm ALL THE WAY UP.

With the Terror Squad in Madison Square Garden at Tito's Trinidad's fight.

Showtime with Team Luis Collazo

After the fight with Luis Collazo
_2005_

Rivera vs Collazo

Jose loses WBA title

Collazo wins split decision

By Bud Barth
TELEGRAM & GAZETTE STAFF

WORCESTER — Maybe Jose Antonio Rivera didn't feel like he lost, but he sure looked like it.

His right eye blackened and almost swollen shut, his nose bloodied, his face red and swollen and grotesque looking, Rivera was the poster boy for the agony of defeat in his dressing room after 12 grueling rounds against a buzz saw named Luis Collazo.

The Worcester-Auburn welterweight had just relinquished his WBA title on a close, split-decision loss to Collazo before 8,567 heavily pro-Rivera fans last night at a raucous and rollicking DCU Center.

Judges Levi Martinez and Nelson Vasquez scored the bout for Collazo, 115-113. Paul Barry, the lone Worcester judge on the panel, scored it for Rivera, 115-114. The Telegram & Gazette had it 115-113 for Collazo.

After the fight, Boston attorney Tony Cardinale said the WBA will be petitioned for "an immediate rematch" because of what he called a scoring discrepancy. It involved the 12th and final round, which was scored in favor of Rivera by both Barry and Vasquez, as well as the T&G. Martinez, however, gave the round to Collazo. Had he followed the other judges, his final scorecard would have been even, 114-114, and the fight would have ended in a draw, allowing Rivera to retain his title.

"Not taking anything away from Collazo — he fought a good fight — but Jose's the champion," Cardinale

Turn to Rivera, Page D11

After Jose Rivera vs. Luis Collazo

In recovery at the hospital with Luis Collazo.

George Horowitz, CEO and Chairman of Everlast Equipment. Whenever I saw George he gave love to George Lozada, great and humble man.

<u>Rest in Peace - 2005</u>

Official Credentials

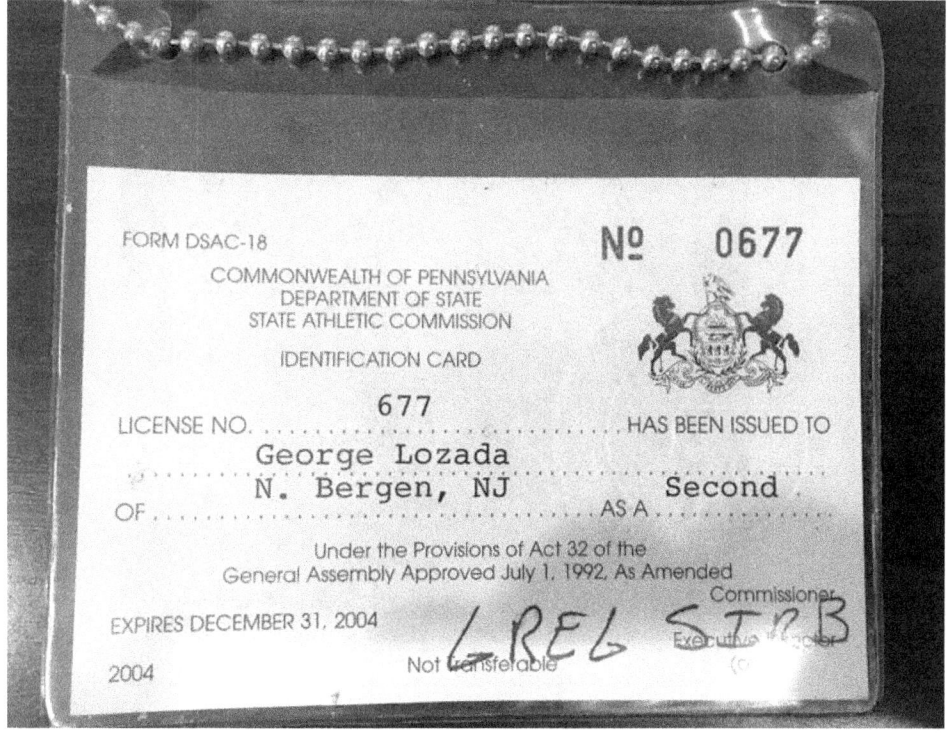

2002 to 2005 – I was getting tired training, coaching, traveling and I wasn't focusing on my business, or my moneymaker. I was manufacturing, distributing to Puerto Rico, Orlando, Miami, and Ft. Lauderdale. I was giving out purchase orders all over the country and it was slowing my money. I was working with *Agapito Sánchez* and on November 15, 2005 he was shot dead in Santo Domingo. It really hurt me that on his comeback he got killed.

I was also working in the corner with Elio Rojas, and I was working with the PAL with Luis Lopez out of Jersey City. I was doing real estate as well. I needed to focus; I didn't want to get caught up in the limelight so I checked myself so I can slow down. I devoted all my time into my business in the real estate. I decided to start just going to the fights at ringside.

Elio 'The Kid' Rojas

Villa Riva, Santo Domingo pura sepa te quiero mucho Spanish Georgie and Moe trainer

Moe, Me, Elio Rojas, Blackmore Trainer & Manager Tony Antineo

Me, Cutman Danny Melendez & Luis Lopez

Agapito Sanchez, Dominican Champion – Rest in Peace

At Gleason Gym in Brooklyn, watching Agapito Sanchez train. Week later he gets killed in Santo Domingo. Chelo and Me will miss you.

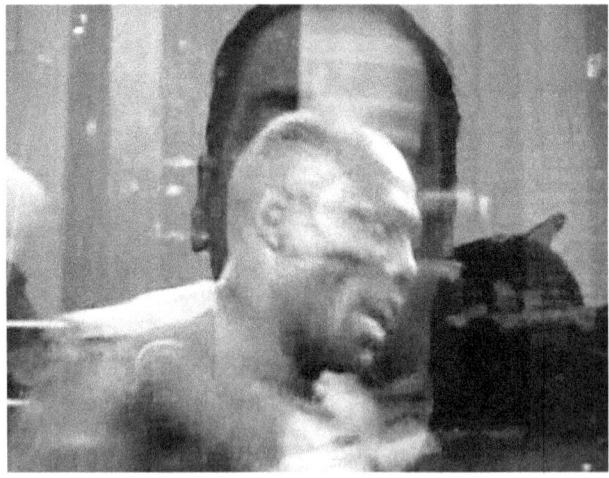

Thinking about Agapito, I had worked real hard that year trying to get him sponsored. I got a couple of attorneys in keller & Williams real estate to back him up, and then a police Sargeant took his life. For weeks and months I felt it in my heart, the pain of a good and loyal friend.

At Elio Rojas fight with Leon Spinks, world champion.

De Puerto Rico, my boy Jose

At the Hunt's Point Market in the Bronx – A&J Produce dock

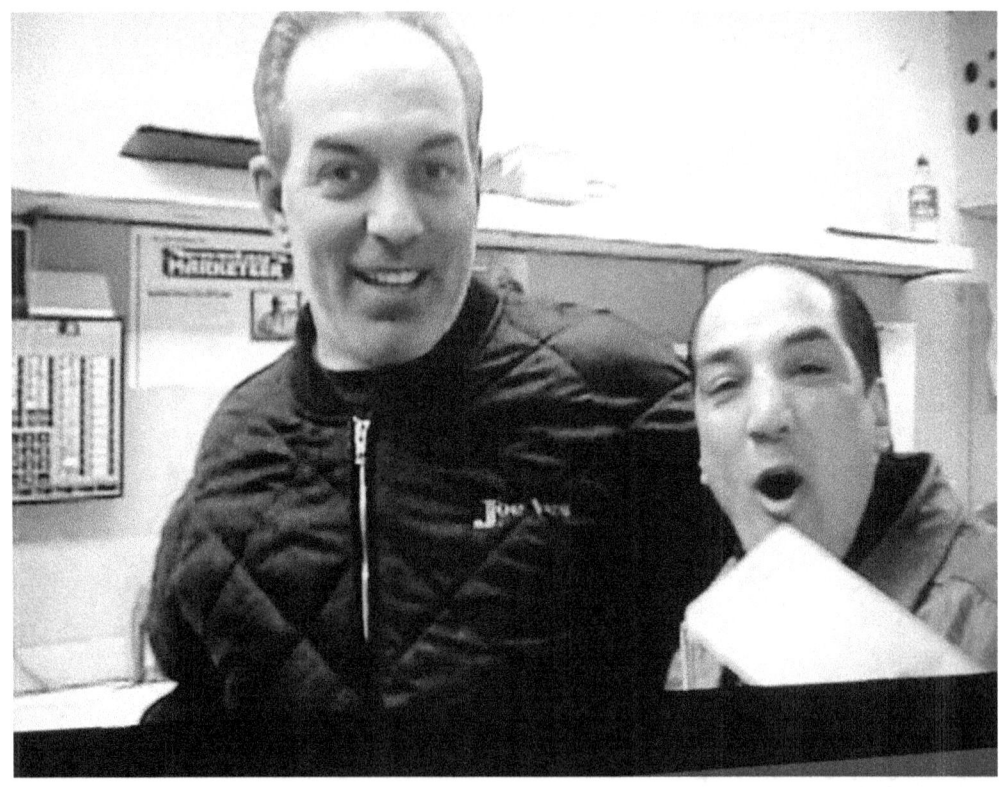

Thank you for the job you gave me when I came home from Sing Sing prison, and I show you my I.D. that I just gotten released and you and Fat Tony gave me a job and put me on the union. I am grateful to A&J produce and my boss Dock & Fat Tony – Italian Power.

That same year in **2005**, I purchased three homes and I moved in to 90 Street in North Bergen. I had a house on 51st Street North Bergen and a house in Weehawken, NJ – I had rented everything out and still selling cleaning products as well as attending to my houses and doing a lot of shoveling in the winter. Having a home isn't so easy as people think; you've got work hard, shovel snow and deal with a bunch of tenants. Going to courts and fighting with tenants in the courthouse because they wouldn't pay the rent, it was all more headache in my life. It's not just having homes, you've got battle sometimes with your tenants in court, its nothing nice.

That's the American dream.

My goal was to eventually go to the shores. My wife had been a good, loyal and faithful wife and she had told me that's all she wanted was a big home close to the shore. I made that my goal. When I was down in dirty, she put up with all my stress. She is a miracle from the Lord. I'm also grateful to my brother for introducing me to her.

Not bad from a prison cell. I just sold my first home, I was excited and we made a little money – I can't say how much but it was enough to buy three other homes and to make my wife a believer in me. My family, once in my life was looking up for me. I wasn't out selling drugs or out late at night and I kept busy. I also wanted to slow down with the boxing, I was getting old and turning 49 the following year, I was tired of going to the Mohegan Sun, going to Vegas and managing Luis Lopez and training with Elio Rojas and dealing with my tenants and new tenants and going to court to try and evict them. I was burned out, but excited.

I just needed to choose my business over boxing and I chose my business. I just wanted to go to the fights now and watch, and focus on my homes and my future. Plus I was going to church regularly, staying faithful to God and to not forget where I come from & remember what God has done for me. This is not a fantasy, it's a true story and definitely God is in my life. Without him I would have still been in prison, so all my glory goes to God - straight up.

"Let no man deceive himself. If any man among you seemeth to be wise in this world, let him become a fool, that he may be wise. For the wisdom of this world is foolishness with God. For it is written, He taketh the wise in their own craftiness. And again, The Lord knoweth the thoughts of the wise, that they are in vain. Therefore let no man glory in men..." 1 Corinthians 3:18-21

Tribute to My Father In Law, Juan Meranges

I will always remember when you were in the hospital with cancer on your last minutes, and you called me over and you said to me "Take care of my girl". I made a promise to you, and I have kept that promise. This is a true testimony. Right about now, I have three houses.

The happiest man in the world, the happiest father in the world. He came from Cuba, he worked night and day to make sure that his daughter got a college degree in the U.S.A. and she did. I've been blessed...

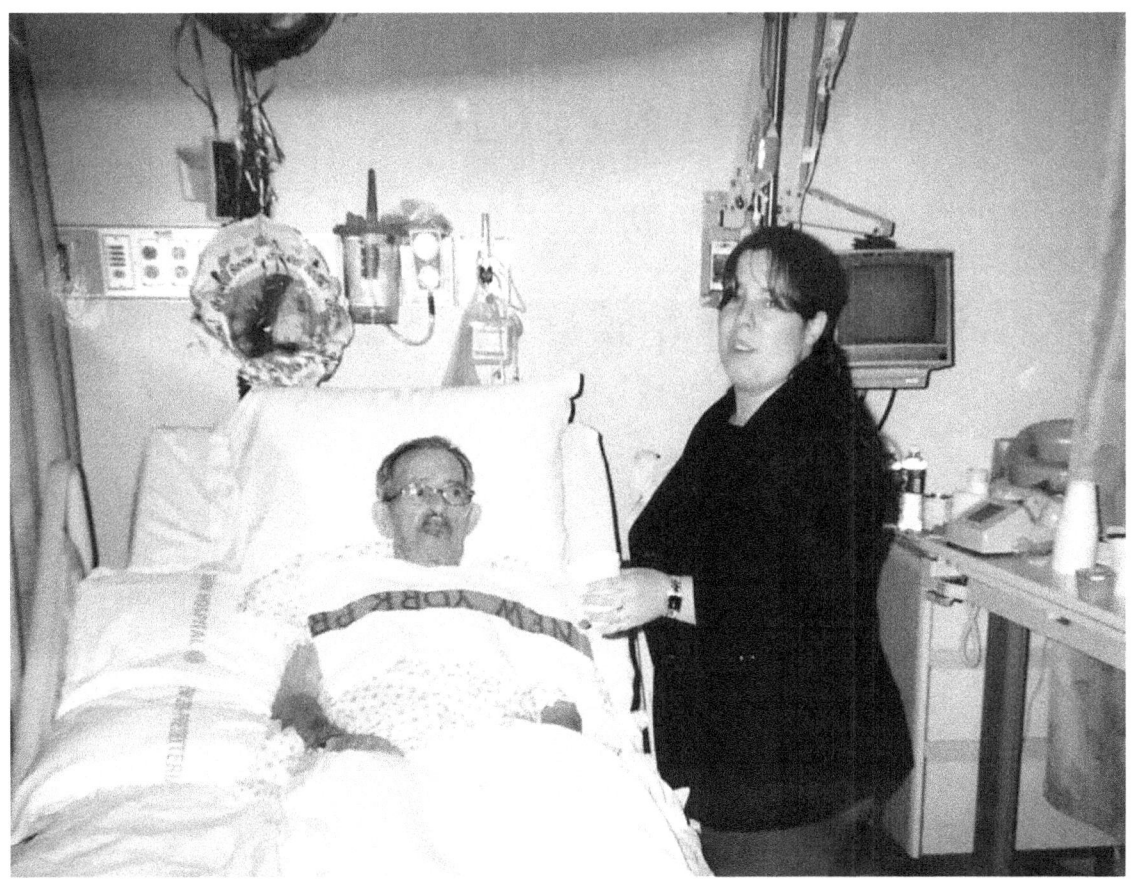

In memory of my father-in-law, passed away of cancer before my daughter was born.

It broke my wife up, she's still broken up years later. She always says he didn't see her granddaughter being born, and that's what haunts her to this day.

If I see my wedding pictures, or I see the videos of my wedding my wife and I will always cry like children.

We truly miss him.

When my daughter was born, I took her to the cemetery and every year after I still take her. I let her know that her grandfather was a good Cuban man. That's what a father does, I give credit where credit is due.

CHAPTER 9
Year 2006

The Birth of My Daughter, a Miracle from the Lord

Only God

Can turn a MESS into a MESSAGE

A TEST into a TESTIMONY

A TRIAL into a TRIUMPH

A VICTIM into a VICTORY

2006, a new chapter in my life and my family where there are no girls, strictly boys – we've all been boys. All my younger brothers have had boys; I'm the oldest out of all of them. The Lord had blessed me with one big miracle, that last thing in my life that I would've expected. My life would change forever, I was pumped then but I was really pumped now for life.

"You are the God who performs miracles; you display your power among the peoples." Psalm 77:14 (NIV)

"Jesus answered them, I told you, and ye believed not: the works that I do in my Father's name, they bear witness of me." John 10:25

"It is better to trust in the LORD than to put confidence in man. It is better to trust in the LORD than to put confidence in princes." Psalm 118:8, 9

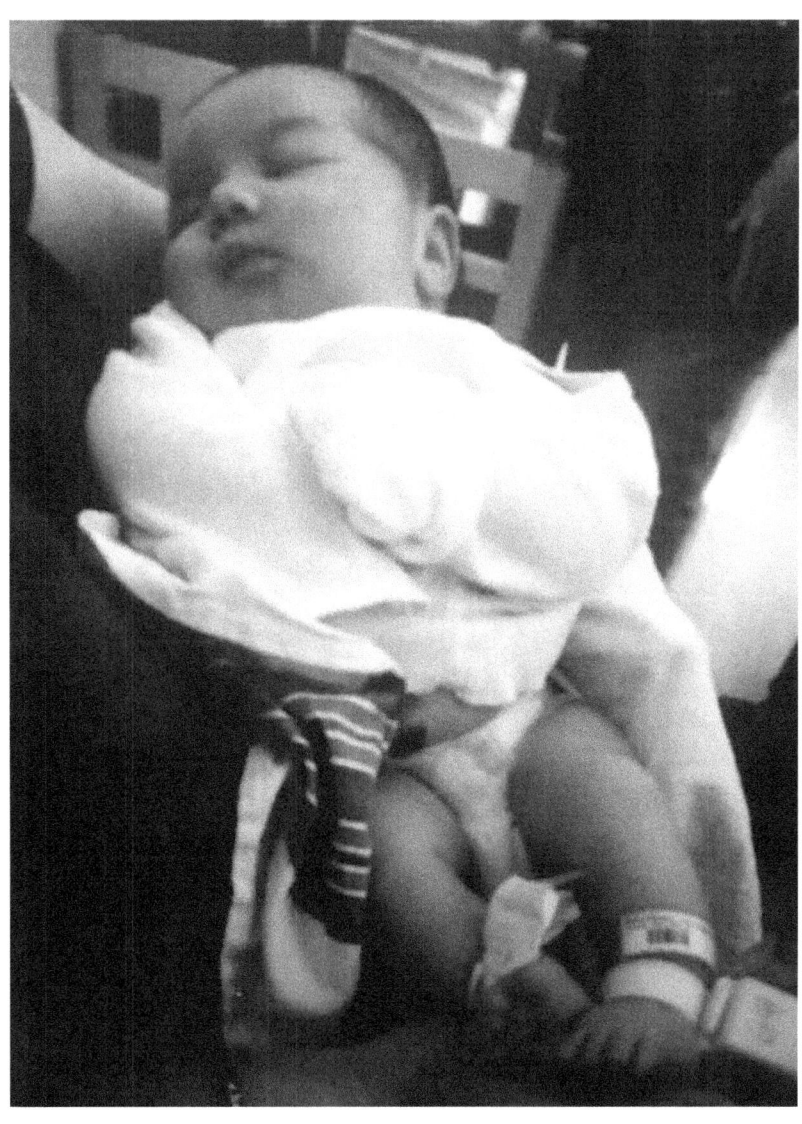

Sarah and Daddy in our new home...

Sarah showing her personality

My daughter was born on **May 5th, 2006** as Sarah Lozada. I took inspiration for the name from the Bible. I spent days trying to get a name for her, my wife and I didn't know what name until one night I got on my knees and asked the Lord "Please, give me a name" and something said open up the bible and look inside. The first thing I saw flashing at me like a flashlight, like a star in the night I saw the name Sarah.

"He hath made everything beautiful in his time..." Ecclesiastes 3:11
Armed & Dangerous

Thank you Jesus, Thank you Lord I am grateful for you.

My angels and Me, I recommend this to everybody.

My titi Minerva, Sarah, Theresa and me. Thank you for coming to see me while I was in prison titi and for your consejos. Sometimes tough on me but, I understand. I still love my family.

Team Sarah and her girlfriends, during Christmas season.

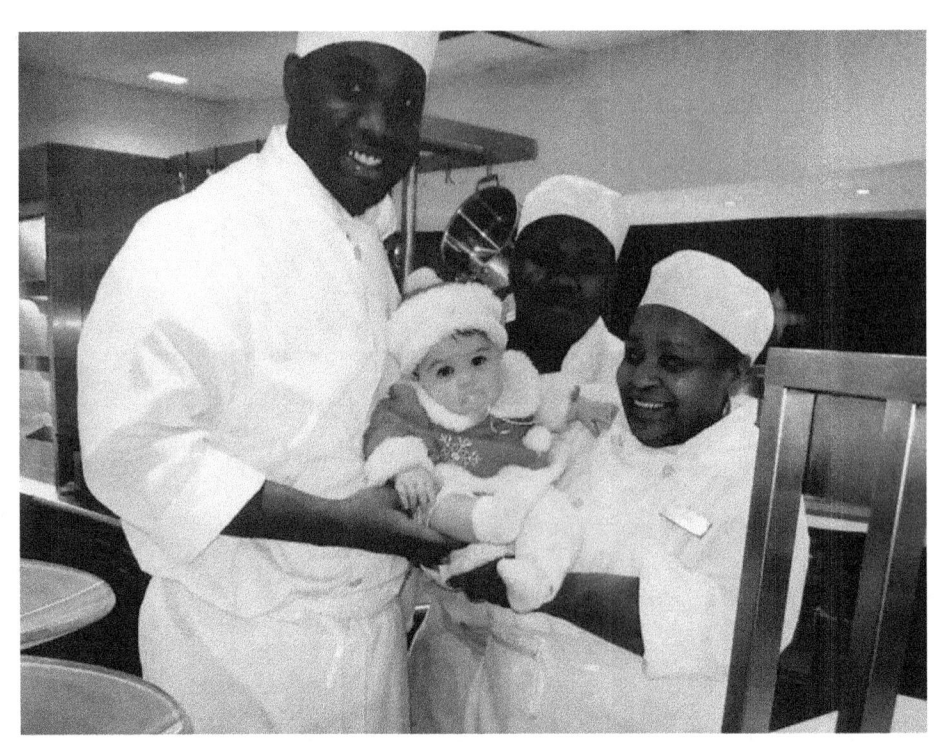

Sarah's Chefs

Sarah Turns One... (2007)

This is a miracle, after all that time I did in the penitentiary for being ignorant, stupid. I am grateful to God that I met him in the penitentiary and he showed me the way. Thank you Lord.

I was at the turkey farm, and I was looking at the turkey's being incarcerated and I shed tears. I felt sorry for them. I wanted to open up the cage and let them out, but I didn't know if they committed a crime.

Sitting at my house looking at my little girl playing around, I was in disbelief that this was happening to me.

I walked into Manhattan Mercedes Benz and I purchased a car for me, and I purchased a car for my girl.

A family get together

Keeping my little girl healthy already

My brother, my daughter and I during Christmas. My brother had just gotten out from the penitentiary. Today he's a man of God and grateful to be out, now living in Spanish Harlem. He's better known as Smokey. While he was incarcerated, I was too and we corresponded back and forth from penitentiary to penitentiary – love letters. I made sure he had commissary money by hitting off my stepmother in the Bronx so she can pay him a visit and put money in his account. His mother did likewise to me and she made sure I had money in my account. Esther Montalvo ~ R.I.P.

Here's my brother packaging a hundred cases of Wonder Products to different restaurants throughout the metropolitan area. I don't' sell crack, I don't sell heroin or any type of drug. I took the negative into the positive. I am CEO of Wonder Products.

  I had just lost my father-in-law, my daughter was born, my wife was back on track focusing on my business and paying the bills. I sold my first house. The Lord was coming around he was answering my prayers. I made a lot of money that I have never made selling drugs or pimping or any criminal activity.

I moved out and moved into the new house and spent about a year there, going to the fights, selling cleaning products and going to church. I was going to Brooklyn Tabernacle often on the weekend. I was also traveling to Florida to go testify inside the prison system to inmates. I would talk about my past experiences as a criminal, and what I am doing after and what God has been doing to me. I don't want to sound all Christian, but the truth will set you free (John 8:32). 2007

I had thirty days to move out after I sold the house. I had to put everything in temporary storage, all of my tv's, equipment, books, clothes, everything. I couldn't believe this was happening in my life but I was excited, and I was clean. God has really done the right thing with me, I have never been this happy before.

"Work hard and become a leader; be lazy and never succeed" Proverbs 12:24, TLB

During the construction of my house

2007

I had to move into my mother-in-law's apartment on 177th Street in Washington Heights until my house was built (as seen above). I had to wait at least another 7 or 8 months for the construction to finish.

I kept working at the PAL Boxing with Evan Rodriguez, my heavyweight that later on in life was signed by Miami Dolphins in 2013. He got a couple of a mil from the deal, I truly believe he could've been a good heavyweight – he was good with his hands. I was so mad at him because I knew his potential at the PAL, but he wanted to go football. I always kept in contact with him and showed him love regardless. My wife and I were excited for him; I would start watching him on TV when he was playing for Miami.

Finally, I moved into my new house with my daughter and wife and I rented the upstairs apartment to the godfather to my daughter, Sammy, the owner at the time of Tipico Restaurant on 177 St. Broadway & his nephew P.J. son of the famous Felix Cabrera. I started focusing more on my business, selling cleaning products and focusing on my daughter as well as backing away from the boxing business. I was now a daddy and I wanted to be the best daddy in the world. I was very worried; I wanted someone that if anything would happen to me they could take care of my daughter.

When I finally met Sammy Cabrera, he was living upstairs and I saw him work night and day around the clock like a bull, like a real Dominican does. I had my eyes on him for six months until one day I told my wife I want Sammy to be the godfather to my daughter and I want my criminal attorney at law Christina Rivera to be the godmother. I got enough courage to walk into another restaurant that he had called 'Casa de Mofongo' and I pulled him over, with tears in my eyes and I said, "I need to talk to you." He always called me 'bori, he never called me Georgie and I said to him "I want you to be the godfather to my daughter."

His eyes lit up, he replied "Me?! Why me 'bori…" and I said, "Because you are a respectful, hard-working, pura sepa Domicano that has no bad habits like drinking or drugs and you always showed me love."

I then approached my attorney Christina Rivera and said, "Would you be the godmother to my daughter" and she replied quick and swiftly, "It would be an honor" and I started tearing up again, I knew that I had made a real good choice in my life. God forbid something would ever happen to my wife or me; I would have Sammy and Christina down and dirty.

Flash-Forward 2009, My Daughter's Baptism

My daughter and the priest

Godfather to my daughter, Sammy witnesses the baptism…

Christina Rivera, the godmother and Sammy Cabrera, the godfather

"Lord, you have assigned me my portion and my cup; you have made my lot secure"
*Psalm 16:5, NIV (<u>**TRUST GOD FOR ALL THINGS**</u>)*

My compadre, his wife Evelyn, Christina Rivera (my attorney the godmother), My Daughter Sarah and the best wife in the world Mariela.

My daughter and her Godmother at Lucky Seven Tapas Bar celebrating her Baptism

Another spot that my Godfather runs

Another production by Felix Cabrera, if you need tickets for the concerts let me know – I got the hookup.

If you're true to the game, then take your girl to this spot

Chuleta Kan-Kan – you cannot get this at Riker's Island or Sing Sing or Bronx house of detention

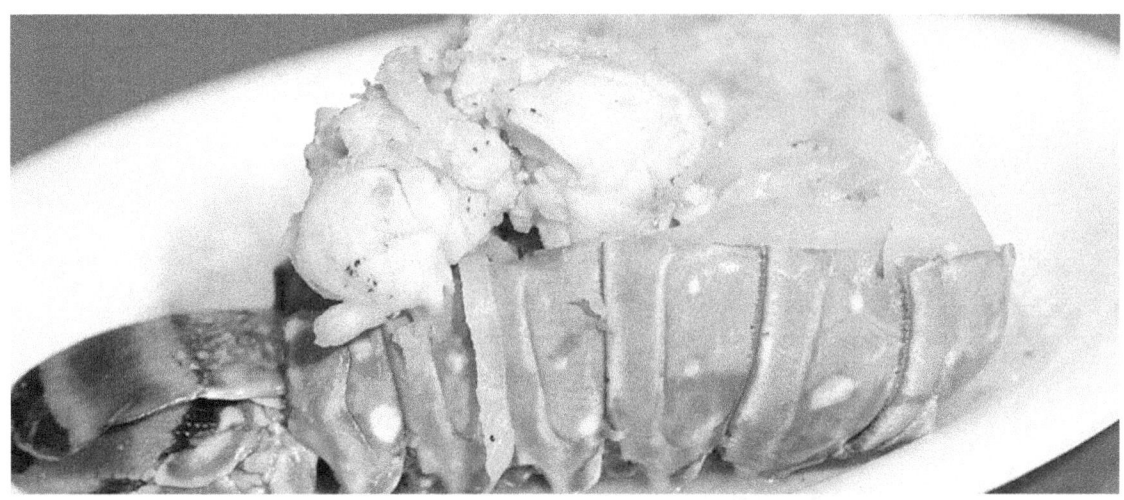

When you come out after doing a couple of years, you can get that. But if you behave and watch your moves you can always have this on the weekends at Lucky Seven. You'll be one lucky guy.

Dominican flan. You have go to Punta Cana or Casa de Mofongo to get some; you can't make those up north doing time…

CHAPTER 10
2010

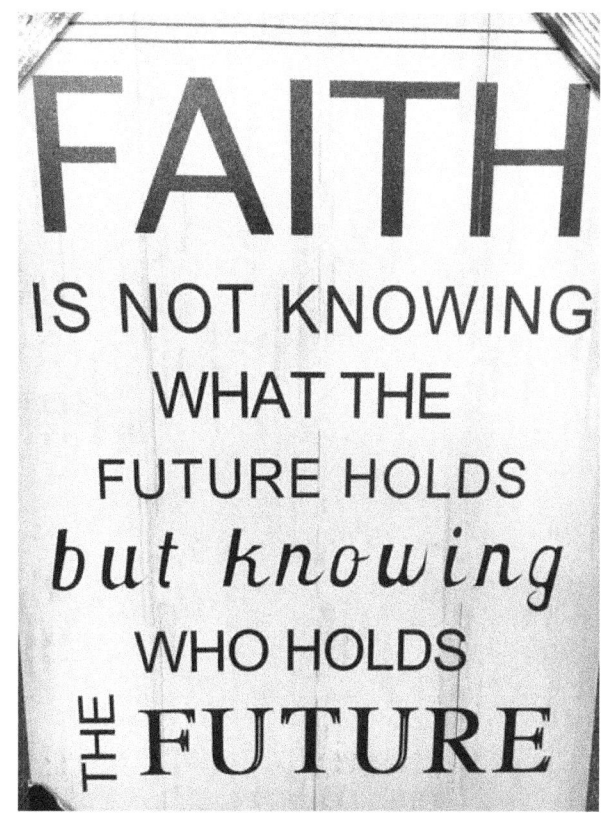

"My protection and success come from God alone. He is my refuge, a Rock where no enemy can reach me. O my people, trust him all the time. Pour out your longings before him, for he can help!" – Psalm 62:7-8, TLB

I moved into my new house finally after spending 7 months living at Washington Heights. I was spending a lot of time in my Godfathers place 'El Tipico' Dominican cuisine restaurant and he purchased 'Casa de Mofongo'.

My daughter, Frankie (manager) workers and me at La Casa de Mofongo. My daughter loves going here, she gets so much attention but most of all she loves the food especially Mofongo con Camarones (shrimp). I taught her how to eat lobsters, and now she's officially hooked. I live to see my daughter smile.

My Godfather's spot in Washington Heights, another production by Felix Cabrera

I would be in this spot 24/7; this spot was bringing in all of the musical artists that Felix Cabrera was producing at the time. All of the Dominican baseball players were showing up too, this place was HOT. Washington Heights was pimping, Dominicans on the map – pura sepa. I didn't just meet Dominicans here at Washington Heights, I met them in Puerto Rico. Dominican's for me weren't new to me; I grew up with them in Puerto Rico. There are plenty of them on the island and they were loyal people. Con sentimientos Buenos. That's why I chose the Godfather to my daughter, a hard-working Dominicano around-the-clock.

I was coming into the city every day with my Mercedes Benz and boxes of cleaning products in the trunk. I would hit all of Jerome Avenue car dealers, I would work Hunt's Point Market until I would sell out then drive to North Bergen, N.J. back to my new home and my little girl & wife. I would bring in mangos from the market, mofongo from la casa – sometimes I would drive to Spanish Harlem and stop on 116th Street to the Cuchifritos spot and pick up pasteles, arroz con gandules, some arcapurias, pastellios de queso y de carne. My wife and daughter would go through the ceiling with all the delicious food I brought back after work.

At the P.A.L. I would meet up with Evan Rodriguez, my heavyweight in the evenings that dumped me for Miami Dolphins for 2 million dollars ☺. I worked with him for about a year and Luis Lopez, and out of Jersey City and Elio Rojas at the Gleason Gym.

From 2010 to 2011, I was working really hard selling my cleaning products and I was saving all of my money because I wanted to move out of North Bergen and buy another house. I had my little girl and I wanted a different atmosphere for my daughter, I wanted to give her a good education. I was spending a lot of money on her Pre-K private child-care. I spent between 2007 and 2009 about $32,400 and from 2009 to 2011 I spent about $18,360 a grand total of **$50,760**.

I had my girl at an early age at Montessori private school and it was *expensive*, but my daughter by the age of 3 was reading and getting an early start at basic math. Every Sunday morning I would go to church and cry out to God thanking him. I made it my goal to stay away from trouble, people, places and things that would get me jammed up and away from my daughter.

Me at New Hope church in Trenton, New Jersey in the hood with Bishop Bonaparte

I would walk around the neighborhoods in Trenton with Dr. Bonaparte and talk to the dope fiends, the less fortunate, and people with no hope. I would try to tell them my life story, sharing all the hardships I went through. I would also fly out every three months to Orlando, Florida to Orange County Prison Ministry and I would go inside the penitentiary and I would use my life story experience and street knowledge & preach about what God has done for me in my life.

This is at the Orange County Prison Ministry annual banquet; I testified that day in front of 300 people.

There were business owners, bankers, police officers, correction officers and more. The bible says 'Don't forget the prisoners'. I promised God that I was always going to use his word to bring up brothers & sisters that were incarcerated & less fortunate. I made it my business to spread the word. Here I am with the prison Chaplain Joseph McGahey and my dear adopted mother Dorothy. They used to wake up early in the morning and take me to work because I didn't have a car.

This family was not a blood family, but a Godly family. My adopted father devoted all his life to preach and be a father at the same time to inmates doing hard time. I am so grateful to God that I had met the McGahey family and I met my papa in prison when I most needed a friend, a father. He stood there firm with me and spoke to me about God. He kept telling me that there was always a tomorrow, and that God was putting me through a test and to trust in God with all of my heart. Which I have done until today, look at me now, a changed man.

Held in the Main Facility Briefing Room

Commit everything in your life to God's care

"What a God he is! How perfect in every way! All his promises prove true. He is a shield for everyone who hides behind him" – Psalm 18:30, TLB.

Wisdom

"The fear of the LORD is the beginning of knowledge: but fools despise wisdom and instruction." – Proverbs 1:7

See, when I go into the penitentiary most of the time I don't go in preaching the word right away. I always talk about my life story and what I've been through, my ups and downs; what the inmates can relate to. My life story: I spent fourteen years in and out of a lot of cells and many penitentiary's. I'm not proud of anything I've done but today I can sit here and look back at 40, 50 years and tell myself I have been a fool – I can accept it.

"A man who refuses to admit his mistakes can never be successful. But if he confesses and forsakes them, he gets another chance." – Proverbs 28,13, TLB

I decided to leave North Bergen and go south, I was focusing more on my daughter. I decided to buy a house 60 miles away from the city, all the way down to the shores.

One day we were by the shores and my little girl told me "Daddy, I want to move by the shores and have a biiiiiig house and a biiiiiig yard" and I responded, "We will". I got on my knees that night and I focused my mind on God faithfully, and I said, "Lord I need help my daughter wants a big house, I want to work as hard as I can to bless my daughter's wishes. It's not about me anymore, it's about my girl and my wife."

"Honor the Lord by giving him the first part of all your income, and he will fill your barns with wheat and barley and overflow your wine vats with the finest wines" – Proverbs 3:9-10, TLB

Acquire blessings and wealth only according to God's plan

"Blessed is the man who finds wisdom, the man who gains understanding….Long life is in her right hand; in her left hand are riches and honor" – Proverbs 3:13,16, NIV

"To be wise is as good as being rich; in fact, it is better. You can get anything by either wisdom or money, but being wise has many advantages" – Ecclesiastes 7:11-12, TLB

In **2011**, I started going by the shores talking to different real estate agents regarding the school districts, which was my largest concern. How much the mortgage was, I really didn't care because my plan was to sell the two houses I had and use the money for the down payment of my million-dollar home. I was looking at the 2-3 million dollar homes but my money wasn't right so I had to stay under, but for now this wasn't bad. It was better than being on Riker's Island or Sing-Sing, wasting my life away. I wanted to go straight in my life and I needed God in my life.

Everything I was doing was becoming like a puzzle, I wish I knew what I know now from an early age. I had to spend almost 14 years out on my life of being stupid and ignorant, having no coaches around me to pick me up in times of needs.

"Fear of man is a dangerous trap, but to trust in God means safety" – Proverbs 29:25, TLB

I always trusted man, father figures from the hood who would give me a gun one time to kill somebody. That's not from God, there's nothing holy or Godly about that. Trust no man, trust God.

"In God I trust; I will not be afraid. What can man do to me?" –Psalm 56:11, NIV

I have traveled to Vegas many times, to watch the biggest fights, I been there done that. I sold drugs, had prostitutes, spent time after hours coked up out of my mind until the next day. What a waste of time that was. Now that I sit outside from a prison cell after many years, and I look into the eyes of my little girl – *I want to live for her.* Give her a fair fighting chance in this cruel world. Please lord; forgive me for my sins and thank you for everything you've done in my life. I am grateful to you Lord.

I've been in the hood; I was born in the hood. I've got my rep sheet that speaks for itself: 'The truth will set you free'. I ain't telling you any lies my brother, trust in God. When you get released after doing your 5, 6, 7, 8 years step up your game in a different lifestyle because 99% of the time you wind up doing time again, and again. I'm a proven fact of that. This is a documentary of my life, a true story.

I finally purchased my 1.3 million dollar home...

A blessing.

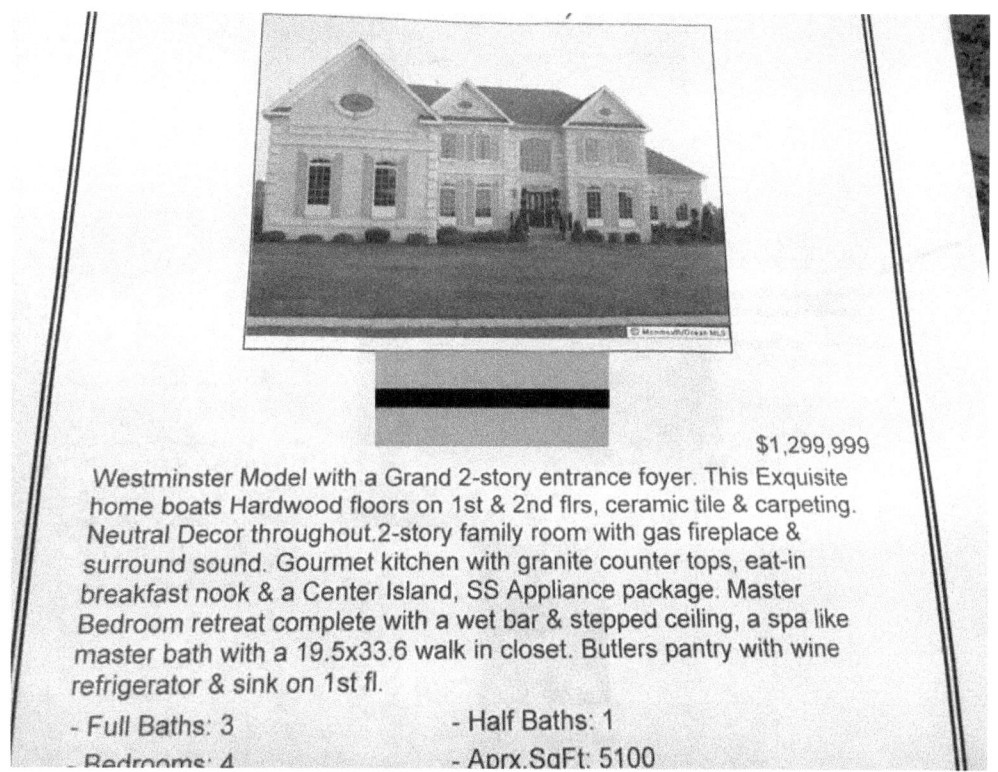

I was like a baby, born again – it wasn't a dream, I wasn't fantasizing and I wasn't faking it to make it. This was a dream come true and I was just getting started.

BORN AGAIN

"That which is born of the flesh is flesh; and that which is born of the Spirit is spirit." – John 3:6

I once didn't believe in God, I use to curse God especially when I was in the cell. I would curse him out, call him out, blame him but and the more I did time I met OG's doing 50 years or 100+ to life who would tell me: "You better turn to God, before you stay here for the rest of your life".

Now here I am doing time on the streets, attending church, squared up and being a real daddy to my little girl. I did time, people say they do time but time did me. I wasted fourteen years out of my life in and out of prisons, and I was done. I wanted to live a normal life. It doesn't mean I still don't go and visit the hood, most definitely I come down to Spanish Harlem, Puerto Rico, Santo Domingo, Orlando, Kissimmee, Washington Heights… I'm from the streets, I'm a true testimony and I need to be on the streets in the hood, down and dirty. I don't want to trip, got to stay true to the game. Don't forget where you come from.

I let them all know what God has done for me – **IN THE HOOD.**

In Washington Heights, the real hood with the latest California Ferrari 2012. Don't hate, participate.

You see my little girl with me; she's always with me. She's my partner in crime and was having fun that day – she was excited. We were on the turnpike together and went to midtown.

To fill it up ☺ it's $68 dollars, super gas. There's no time to smoke crack around here bro.

Finally moving into my new crib by the shores in central New Jersey, two blocks away from my church and an excellent school district. My daughter was excited and my wife was living it, a dream come true for her. I proved everybody in my life wrong; they didn't want me to marry my wife because I was from the hood, an ex-con. But they didn't know how I was Godly, that I was a changed man and that we should have a second chance in life. I didn't choose this society, this society chose me.

But then again, I get up at 6 o'clock in the morning. I make pancakes and eggs for my wife and daughter. I used to do it for the prisoners many years ago at the mess hall, but now I do it for my girls. I take ten cases of cleaner and I go out and sell them, making a thousand a day. I don't have to sell crack, coke, heroin or pills and screw people's life up; God is good, trust in me. I'm that testimony.

At Christmas in my new home

Thank you God, I'm the happiest man in the world. I'm blessed. I trust in you.

Daddy cooked for the family in our new mansion

I had to get a purebred bluenose pit-bull because there were foxes in my backyard and I wanted my daughter to be protected at all times. I also have 12 security cameras around the house, but it's not effective against wild animals.

My daughter was so happy with her new house, she was so excited she was out in the country watching horses, pumpkin picking during October and watching the deer cross our house.

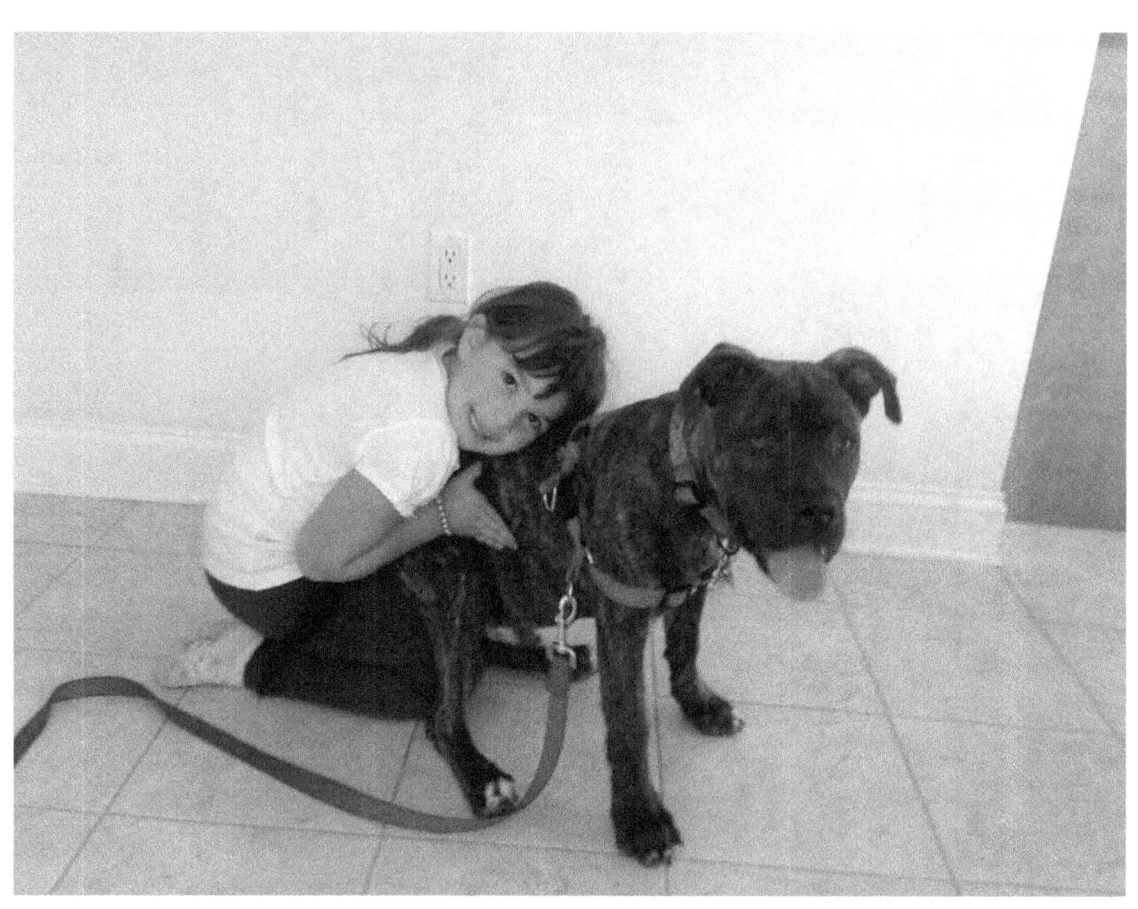

Two months later, look at his paws...

I enrolled my daughter in extracurricular activities such as Self-Defense programs

At the Englishtown, NJ Raceway Track

I do anything to keep my daughter's smile on her face

If this doesn't motivate your life to go on and live and be a good citizen, pay your bills, keep a family – I promise you that you won't regret reading about my documentary. People, places and things will always keep you behind bars. Rest dress and do the best but work hard.

Sarah at the house practicing with me her kick strikes

Thank you Lord for my son and my daughter, father you've been so good to me – I am grateful to you. I cannot ask God for anymore, I just want to help the unfortunate people behind bars. I'm not trying to show off, I just found a way to live a better life. I could do better by doing right. I am a true testimony.

My son is getting bigger and my daughter is enjoying every minute of it. She's one happy little girl and I want to be the best father in the world. I didn't do all that time in the pen for nothing, I got something out of it. I hope you do too when you get out.

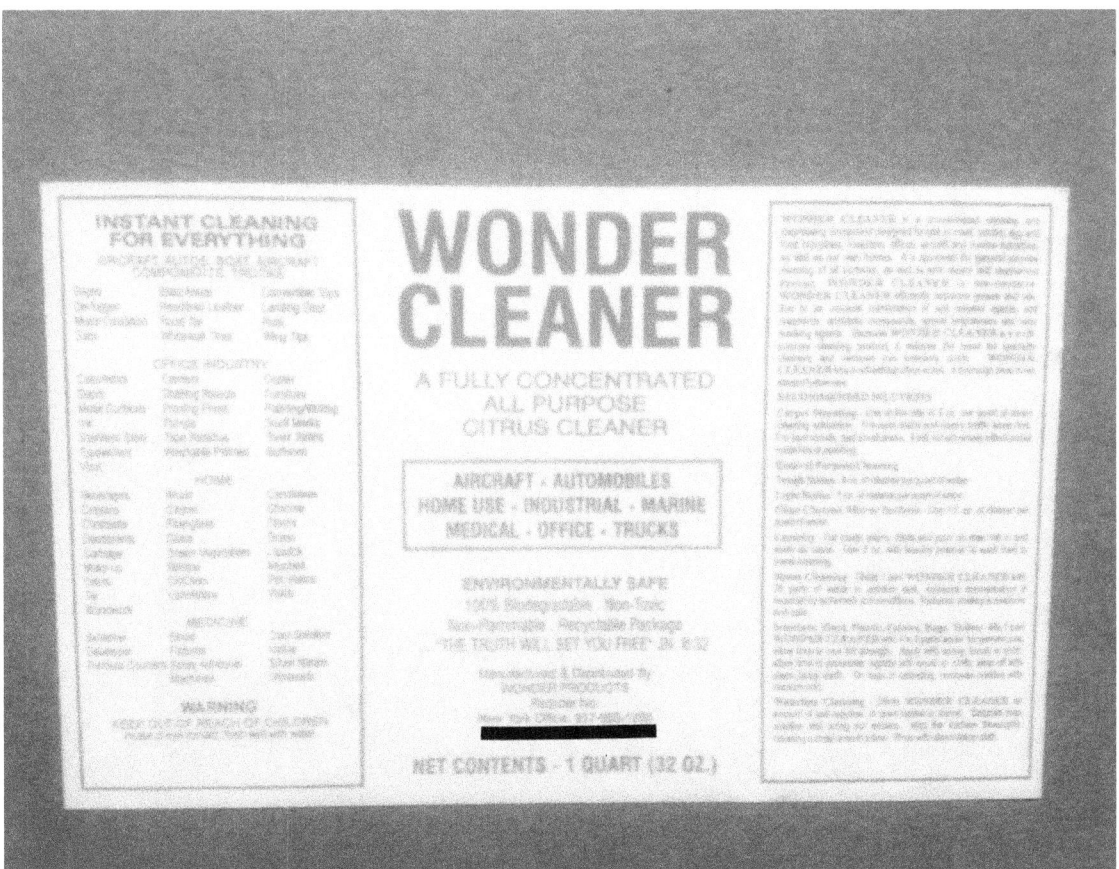

Between **2011 and 2012** I took my business to another level. I started doing more hospitals, more corporate offices, purchase orders, etc. I never knew that someday I would be the C.E.O. of a corporation, of manufacturing and distributing my own cleaning products. I also manufacture oven and grill degreasers, air fresheners, citrus products, tire shine, bleach and currently I'm working on a formula for disinfectants trying to get my licenses. I hope and pray to God that whoever reaches my book and reads will use my experience as a tool for you to be successful and gain knowledge about my life experience. Everything is possible through God.

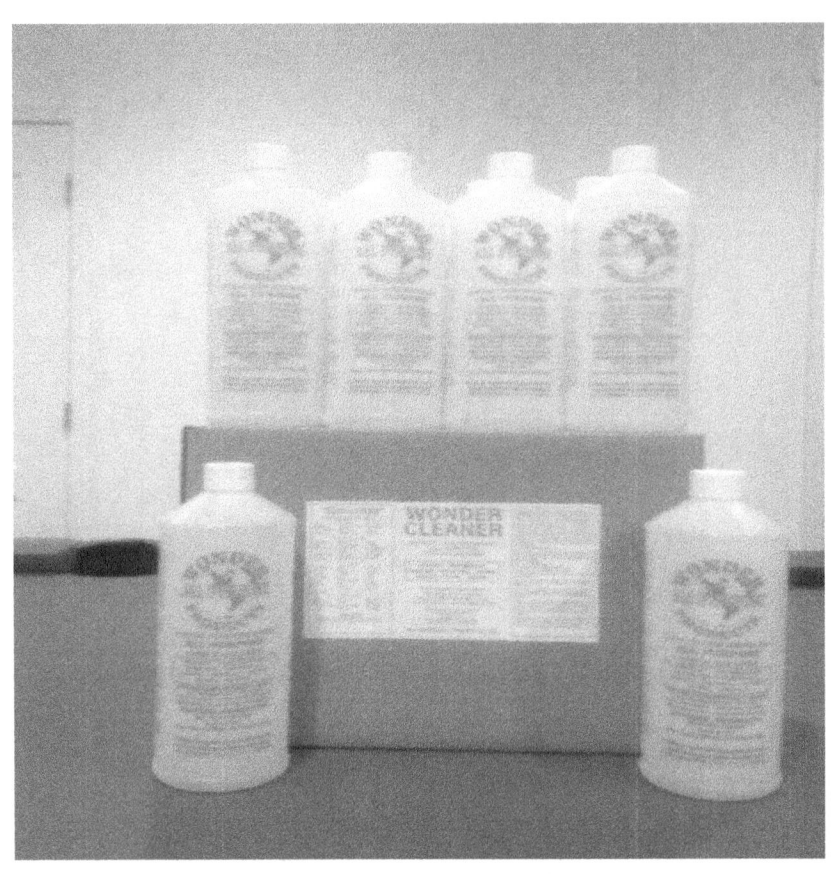

I only sell it by the case, 12 in a case at $144 for the case.

You buy two cases at $288; I throw in a case for free. That's how I make my money.

I also have 55-gallon drums at $1,200 per drum of fully concentrated all purpose cleaner. I sell two a day and I'm good.

"All who humble themselves before the Lord shall be given every blessing, and shall have wonderful peace" – Psalm 37:11, TLB

"Let us not become weary in doing good, for at the proper time we will reap the harvest if we do not give up." – Galatians 6:9, NIV

Back in 2007 I was sitting on a two-seater Mercedes and the chief of police hit me in the back. I had to undergo surgery and I couldn't walk for about a year, but I was just going through a test and I turned to God again. Another testimony in my life, I could've been dead but life chose me instead.

"I have confidence in you through the Lord" – Galatians 5:10

I didn't work the streets for about a year, I only did deliveries. A year later I was selling a lot of cleaner than the year before, my phone was ringing 24/7 for re-orders. I had to hire people to help me; sometimes I would work until 10 o'clock at night making deliveries. Work hard, play hard through God everything is possible.

Another test in my life was when I lost my uncle Papo Crespo in 2012; he was like a father figure to me when I was in Puerto Rico. He was my friend, my brother, and my father – Rest In Peace, Juan Crespo.

I'll see you when I get there Tio. I'm going to heaven to meet you.

CHAPTER 11

Our Friendship

"I have learned that to have a good friend is the purest of all God's gifts, for it is a love that has no exchange of payment" - Frances Farmer

On November 20, 2012 around 7 p.m. Camacho was shot in the jaw

I got a call from one of my homeboy's from Spanish Harlem that Hector Macho Camacho had been shot in Puerto Rico and I was stunned. I was in disbelief, the first thing I did was tell my wife to book me a plane ticket to San Juan, Puerto Rico. I called Ismael Leandry, and I didn't have any contact with the family until I touched down in Puerto Rico.

EL EXMANEJADOR y amigo personal de Macho Camacho, Ismael Leandry, estuvo en el Centro Médico en todo momento.

I hooked up with Ismael and I got information on Camacho's condition.

PESAR. El doctor Ernesto Torres luce compungido al conversar con u[n] de los presentes ayer en el Centro Médico.

I spoke to Dr. Torres and all I wanted to know was if he was going to make it.

A little politics between the doctors opinions; I wasn't any doctor so I had no opinion and it wasn't my place to say, it was the families. I was just there for the support and because Macho had been faithful to me through the years.

I was listening to the conversation between Doctor Torres and Ismael, and right then and there I was getting flashbacks from Vegas and Miami to Puerto Rico about all the good times I had with the Camacho family. I will always treasure this experience with the champ of the world; I couldn't believe what I was listening to from the doctor.

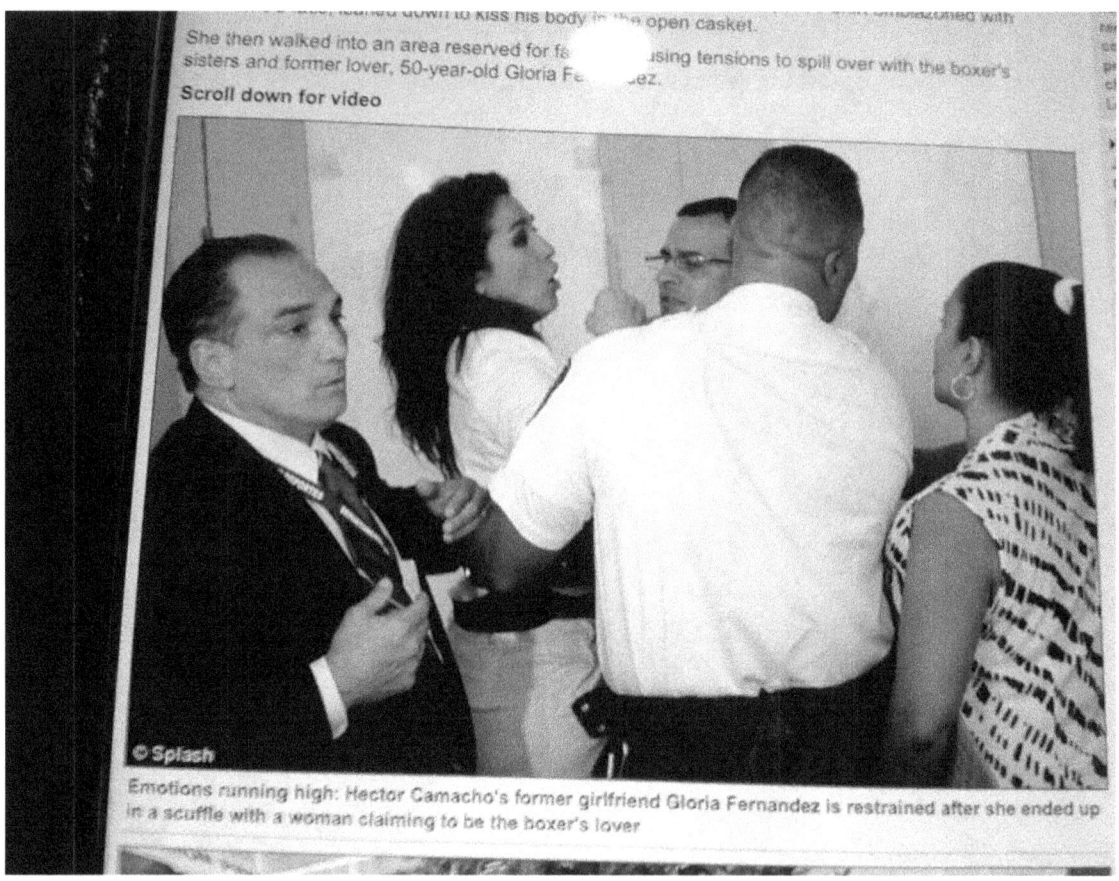

I got caught in the middle of a fight which in the past running with Camacho through the year, I've seen plenty of fights. I was saying to myself, "What's going on here?!"

Macho with the former President of the United States, Ronald Reagan. Exclusive picture never seen before, this picture was given to me by Ismael Leandry. When he gave me the picture I cried out loud. I thought about when I was on the streets cracked out of my brain and Macho always told me to look for God.

Once Sugar Ray said to me, "Georgie, this is one fight I should have never taken."

Camacho's mother and me. I will always respect her & admire her for being such a good mother. I never had a mother like that, she would always show me love. If I ever offended the family in my way of being crazy Georgie, I apologize to them.

Alex Sanchez a.k.a. "El Nene" and me at Camacho's wake.

Puerto Rico's best 'Wilfredo Benitez', a former Puerto Rican professional boxer and the youngest world champion in the sport's history.

I was trying to find out which one was single ☺ I'm only kidding. I was making them laugh as the Joker that I am. I had shed tears the day before and that morning I saw him. A couple of years ago I had also lost my good friend Agapito Sanchez the boxer

and I had lost my baby sister that year too. It's okay to cry but you've got to also smile and go on with life. I spent 14 years of my life crying in a cell.

Ismael Leandry and me. It's been a pleasure and an honor having a faithful friend. I'm going to miss you Hector but I will always remember in Orlando, Florida you always said to me "Look for God" and the good advice you passed onto me. That's a true friend.

Hector Camacho and I would always take pictures like this with cops, but because he wasn't there this is how we did it instead – showtime! Before your newjacks.

Ismael said to me "Georgie, these are Camacho's people" Hogar Crea in Puerto Rico.

Inside J.C. towers in Puerto Rico, me, Camacho jr. and Ismael & some tourists.

Tito Trinidad, Georgie, Ismael and the man of the hour the father of Tito Trinidad, Felix. We were doing Telemundo Live talking about the experience with Hector Camacho.

Making everybody laugh like always, backstage at Telemundo.

It's Macho Time

Inside Telemundo with Evan Calderon y la reportera

Ismael talking about Camacho's stories in his boxing career

A sad day for Puerto Rico

On 106th Street in Spanish Harlem talking to the reporter Gelena Solano, asking me questions about losing my good friend.

When she was asking me questions, I had to turn away. I lost history in my heart.

      I recall many years ago when I first came home from the penitentiary, after doing some hard time for murder in the first degree after a home invasion the first person that came to East 110th Street in Spanish Harlem was the champ Hector Macho Camacho. He was in a black convertible Porsche and he had one of those big 007 James Bond phones from the 80's. Everybody in the neighborhood was taking pictures of him and there was a mob of people downstairs. People were calling me out the window by my name until I finally looked down and I always used the quote: "Pimping ain't easy" That same day Camacho took me shopping and we went to Copa Cabana on 60th Street and from there we went to the after hour.

He was always preaching to me, he sounded like a preacher from church. He was so godly, people didn't really know that side of him – he was truly a Christian. The problem with him was he had blessed a lot of people and some friends didn't appreciate it. But I am a true testimony that I was loyal to him, and he was loyal to me. Rest in peace my brother and I'll always love you bro, and miss you.

CHAPTER 12
2013

In 2013 my daughter was 7 years old and I was attending church hard and working really, really hard. Between the mortgage, my three unit central air conditioner in my house, my three electric car garage, my Direct TV, FIOS, $20,000 a year taxes, and even my garbage that I have to pay to be picked up as well as having my daughter taking flute, vocal, drama classes and Kumon Math Academy plus my GL-450 – now who's going to flip this bill, monthly? Me.

I'll get up every morning like I was incarcerated in the prison system, as if I were going to the mess hall at 3:30 to work the line for the inmates for a dollar a day. I prefer to get up, square up, play my bunk like a punk, turn to God and go out every day selling cleaning products, which I had done now for the past 20 years, plus flipping homes and shoveling snow. When I see my little girl and I look in her eyes, I say to myself I am one of the luckiest guys in the world. Not everybody has a second chance. Most of all of my homeboys are in Attica or Sing Sing prison, or at Saint Raymond Cemetery dead. I'm the last man standing.

Last man standing with my daughter at the park.

Most of the old-timers that I've met doing hard times, they always said to me: "The hardest thing to do time is when you cannot be with your little girl, your kids, or your family". That's horrible, and that's why I chose this square life. That doesn't mean I won't go to the big fights at Madison Square Garden or Vegas, but you won't find me up in no clubs at 2-3 o'clock in the morning. I've got a little girl to come home to.

For this, I would work day and night if I had to and to bring the bread and butter home to my family. I don't have to sell drugs or do illegal things.

I recall doing 23 hours in a cell and I would call out to God that I had enough, that this isn't the life that I want for me. Trust me, we all get soft when you find yourself in the dungeon with no mail, no visits, no phone calls and no outside contact.

"I sought the Lord, and he heard me, and delivered me from all my fears." – Psalm 34:4

"Do not be anxious about anything, but in everything, by prayer and petition, with thanksgiving, present your requests to God. And the peace of God, which transcends all understanding, will guard your hearts and your minds in Christ Jesus." – Philippians 4:6, 7 (NIV)

At Church with my daughter every Sunday and giving thanks to God for the miracle that he's done in my life to turn around.

PRAYER

"The eyes of the Lord are on the righteous and his ears are attentive to their cry; the righteous cry out, and the Lord hears them; he delivers them from all their troubles. The Lord is close to the brokenhearted and saves those who are crushed in spirit." – Psalm 34:15, 17, 18 (NIV)

"And all thing, whatsoever ye shall ask in prayer, believing, ye shall receive." – Matthew 21:22

The bible says ask and you shall receive, I always asked God for money. Don't believe that God won't do you right, as long as you're on the right path I guarantee you the Lord will give you some money.

"Be careful for nothing; but in every thing by prayer and <u>supplication</u> with thanksgiving let your requests be made known unto God." – Philippians 4:6

<u>Supplication</u> – *the action of asking or begging for something earnestly or **humbly**.*

I don't want anyone in the world to misunderstand me that I'm using the word of God and Christianity to prosper in my life. I'm only using the tools that are in front of me, I do have to send my girl to college.

Who's going to pay for her dance classes?

Who's going to pay for her horse riding & pumpkin picking? ☺

Each pumpkin is about $50 bucks

That day I spent about $250 in pumpkins just to make my girl happy

$250 for pumpkins so that the birds can eat them ☺ but anything to make my girl happy. It's better than doing time in the penitentiary, trust me.

Later that year in April, I was invited to attend my Godfather's wedding. He was getting married in Punta Cana at the Melia Caribe Tropical an all-inclusive beach & golf resort. I have never been in Punta Cana so I was excited to go with my family.

On Saturday, April 23rd 2013 I arrived at La Republica Dominicana, I was very excited and I have never been to this beautiful island of working and honest people.

Republica de Santo Domingo at the airport

We were waiting for the mob squad to come pick us up and bring us to the hotel, El Melia

What a beautiful place, this was the entrance. Dominicans are not only popping at Washington Heights, they're also popping at Santo Domingo. A great experience for a New Yorker like me.

When they told me that it was going to be $900 dollars a day with all food & drinks included, I said I'm in and my wife was really happy that we were going on vacation and a wedding

This island was massive and beautiful; we were ready to head to the pool

I started speaking English to him, and he said "Bori, habla me en espanol que tu save, que tu no eres gringo"

Having a mamajuana in Santo Domingo by the pool

Don't think that because I have a smile here that times like this when I'm enjoying myself and I'm in the world outside looking in that I don't get any flashbacks.

Freedom is worth every penny.

"Life will be brighter than noonday, and darkness will become like morning." – Job 11:17

La combination perfecta, I will take this moment with my daughter to the grave

My testimony

"I tell you the truth, he who believes has everlasting life." – John 6:47

My little girl is driving us around the island; the captain gave her the steering wheel

I'm in heaven

My wife was having a blast, she deserved that and more. She's a good wife and good mother.

God is good all the time, not sometimes

My girl and I

My wife, my daughter and myself at the resort

No te equivoces papa, you know what it is

Street bosses

Los millionarios ☺

Washington Heights

My compadre which I adore, he's been a friend & faithful & and his wife Emilia

La boda de ella tiene que ser la major

Having a great time at the wedding

We are having a great time

Taking a selfie

What a blast

"...to love his neighbor as himself, is more than all whole burnt offerings and sacrifices." – Mark 12:33

It's not what we offer up, but what we think of our fellow man that impresses God. Money without mercy is meaningless.

On the way back home on the airplane, I started crying. My wife asked me what was wrong with me that I was crying. I said to her, "This is the first time in my life that I really appreciate my freedom and the time that I spend with you and my daughter in Punta Cana, Santo Domingo."

CHAPTER 13

In 2013, my heavyweight from P.A.L. Boxing, Evan Rodriguez cost me a couple of million dollars. When I first met him, I knew he could've been the champ of the world. I knew he was somebody; he was 6 ft. 2 in and weighing about 240 lbs, fast with his hands, he reminded me of Mohammed Ali. I was so excited of him, I was thinking about the Olympics and gold medals, going pro and getting a big payday with a heavyweight.

But he dumped me with love. I was never mad at him because he did what he wanted to. After I spent money on his Everlast shoes and clothes, I wanted to be his trainer and manager at the same time. I was daydreaming because I always wanted to have a heavyweight.

His professional football career began with the Chicago Bears in 2012, signing a 4-year contract then released on June 10, 2013. He dumped me for the millions ☺.

Then on June 11, 2013 he was signed by the Miami Dolphins for more digits. I probably would have dumped myself too for that kind of money. Later on November 4, 2013 he was signed on with Buffalo Bills. He has advanced with his career with Tampa Bay Buccaneers and more recently in 2016 Lehigh Valley Steelhawks.

I lost contact with him for about a year, almost two years. I didn't hear from him until one day I walked into a grocery store in North Bergen and the owner Jose said to me "Georgie, your boy was just here the NFL football player…" I said to him "Whoa, I missed him but if you see him again give him my card." A few months later I'm on the turnpike, my phone rings and it's my heavyweight Evan Rodriguez.

He started talking to me about God, about how God has been so good to him. I would say to myself, "Am I listening to Evan Rodriguez, the NFL player, my heavyweight?"

Not only was he doing good, he had a good wife and some stacks. I was so happy for him. I said to myself, "God is so good." And God knows Evan needed the help from God. The same week, we went to church, that week we went to eat lobster and shrimp and he was out to Buffalo for training camp. We would talk on the phone constantly and talk about God, exchange scriptures and keep in touch. We would talk almost every day.

God is good, I could see him thinking "I can't believe I'm here..."

Thank you Jesus

I think I was more excited than him and I'm still excited. How a kid from the hood comes up like that. You've been blessed.

Evan was giving back to the community in North Bergen by hosting a youth football camp. I attended with my little girl and she had a blast.

My little girl waiting for her autograph from Evan Rodriguez

Evan Rodriguez with his mother, Frances. She is so proud of her son. That's how I met him, through his mother. She used to go to work everyday walk up the hill on 85th Street in North Bergen. I said to her, "That boys got a future, can I train him in boxing?" I couldn't believe how big he was and so fast. She's been blessed and he's definitely a good son. Tiene sentimientos bueno, he loves his mom. I don't think his father was in his life, just like me. That's why I think we got along so good.

He was even teaching the dogs how to play football ☺ He's a really good guy, I am blessed to have seen him come up.

While I was taking all the pictures and filming him, he said, "Put the camera down, I want to talk to you seriously." And I had no idea what he was going to tell me. I was shocked that he was talking to me in that tone of voice. He put his arms around me and I felt the love that he had for me. He said to me, "You're a great daddy, and you'll always when I was a kid was like a father figure to me. So, my wife is pregnant and I want you to be the godfather to my baby girl." I was "Evan, why me?"

I just wanted to start crying right then and there, because he knows my past. He knows I've been in prison a few times and I had taken somebody's life. I've done time for murder. He said to me, "I don't care about your past. I care about your present, and the way you treat your daughter in a special way and I respect you for who you are OG, and I want you to be the godfather to my daughter. Period."

I said, "Definitely, definitely, definitely yes"

A few months later, Evan told me that the baby had a rare birth defect called 'anencephaly' which resulted in her missing a portion of her brain, scalp and skull. I couldn't believe what he was telling me, I was so sad. I felt like it was my own daughter and I wasn't going to start asking God why. You never ask God why; you accept the reality and trust in God. The first thing I asked him was, "Are you going to have an abortion?" he said "No way, I'm going to put my trust in God."

From an article on The Daily Signal, Evan is quoted saying *"We both have gotten better with the support of family, friends, and parents who have been through it or currently going through it now, and of course our faith in trusting the man upstairs."*

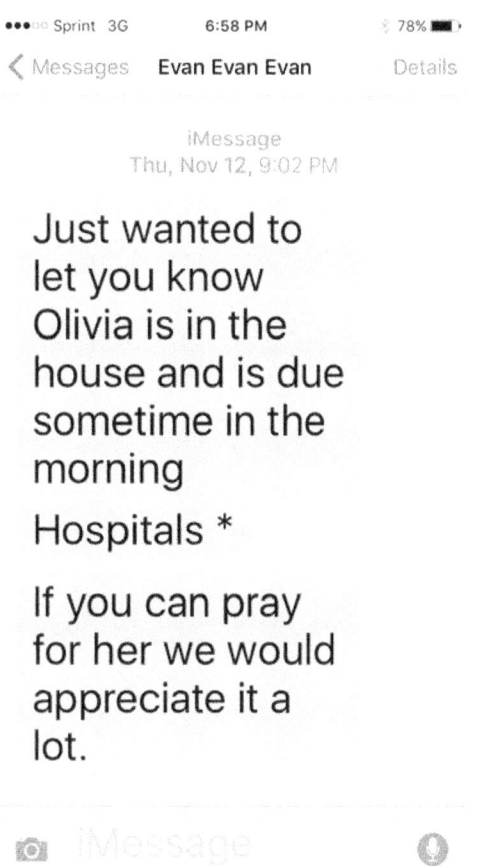

A personal text message from Evan Rodriguez

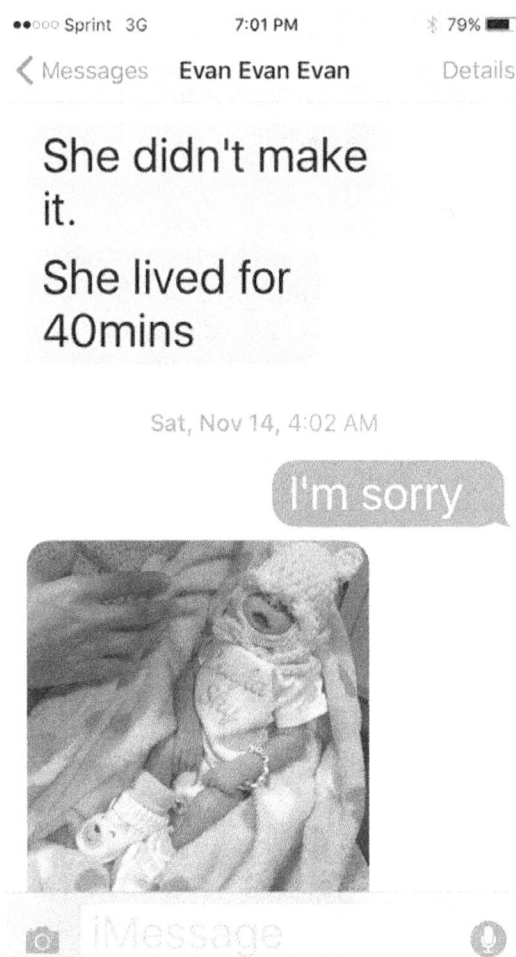

That night, all I was thinking about was my daughter. How grateful I am to God that all the crack, coke, weed and anything I've done in my life that my daughter is healthy. Not only was I crying for me, but I was crying for Evan because he was so excited to be a father. I didn't know what to tell him. I know he was strong and he had been talking godly to me, and he knew it was a test in his life.

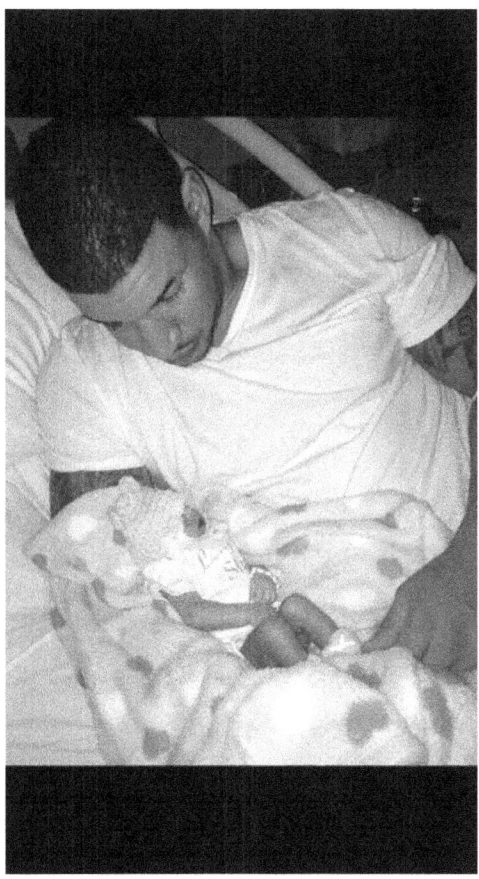

I could just imagine what he was thinking holding his daughter in this moment.

Layla Sky Rodriguez.

I was standing there looking at Layla Sky, she was going to be my goddaughter and I was going to be the best godfather. I was also thinking about my little girl and how God has been so good to me. How grateful can I be to God?

"We can make our plans, but the final outcome is in God's hands" – Proverbs 16:1, TLB

I spoke with Evan after the funeral and I saw that he was a changed man. He would speak about God more than I would and he was attending church regularly, hanging with the pastor. I would call him up or text him and he would be like, "Church up, we here"

I was saying to myself, the Lord has a plan for Evan. I don't know what it is but I feel that the Lord is going to bless him. He deserves it, he's a good kid very respectful and I know he loves God and I know he's not mad at God.

A year later, his wife is pregnant again.

He called me one day for Christmas and said, "My wifey is pregnant. It's a boy". I thanked Jesus and said to myself: He went through a hard test, he passed the test and the Lord has blessed him with a baby boy. He always wanted a baby boy. I believe in miracles.

A few months later, Evan Rodriguez purchased a restaurant & lounge called 'Arena' in Long Branch, New Jersey. I was invited to the superbowl event they had hosting with big baller NFL players.

You see me with Mohamed Sanu, Kashif Moore, Tim Wright, E-Rod Rodriguez, Julian Talley, Derek Dennis, Nick Williams, the million dollar babies. Even if I'm broke I'm around the millionaires, so I'm good to go. The Lord has been good to me.

CHAPTER 14

2015

My true story, my 14 years in state prison I went through it all in my life so far and God has blessed me to become a clean and sober, honest man. I'm an example of hope for all who choose to reinvent themselves and follow a straight, godly path in your life.

You live a good life praising God, praying faithfully, serving God faithfully and trusting in God.

"And I will restore to you the years that the locust hath eaten, the cankerworm, and the caterpillar, and the palmerworm, my great army which I sent among you."

If you feel like you have thrown your life to the wind, take a look at the only one that can make you a winner. He is that author of time and can make up for all that's lost. Take Jesus today and watch him how quickly He can turn things around for you. Only God can take a life of wasted years and defeat and turn it all into victory. Let him!

I'll give you an example of another true testimony in my life…

I did 18 months in Orlando, Florida and I met Chaplin Joseph McGahey, he has given his whole life to the prisoners from Bible books to praying for them & with them, through death of family members. I have met a lot of Chaplins in my time from Sing Sing to the house of detention when I was facing life in prison, but when I met Joseph McGahey I knew he was a true man of God through his actions. When I got out, he went to the prison to pick me up. He had promised me he was going to be at the door when I got out, and when I got out he was there. He's been in my life ever since, that's my father, my papa and my mama Dorothy McGahey. When I first got my job she would wake up at 3:30 in the morning and take me to the job site and she wasn't even my blood mother. He recently had a heart attack and I flew to Orlando and the day that I was flying back to New York I cried on his shoulder for about 20 minutes. I am so grateful to this family.

Papa and mama I will always love you, you know my true testimony and you know my life story. You gave me love and I took off like a rocket. I got married like a promised, I got a little girl, a few homes, I manufacture cleaning products and I am presently starting Lozada Construction, LLC. I want to get into start building homes…

This is a testimony for you to take and run with it. If I can do it, through Christ then anything is possible.

"Be on your guard; stand firm in the faith; be men of courage; be strong."
– 1 Corinthians 16:13

"…the fruit of the Spirit is love, joy, peache, patience, kindness, goodness, faithfulness…"
– Galatians 5:22

FAITH

Just because you're doing 10, 15, 25 years it's a time to check yourself. I know it's not easy, but if you're going to go do time, then time will do you. Do time, that means get your G.E.D., start taking college courses, get a college degree, get a B.A. in Business, in Criminal Justice or Criminal Investigation. Take a course in plumbing.

Do time. Don't let time do you. You can be doing time in the penitentiary and get yourself caught up on a murder or assault charge and wind up doing more time. Do time, don't let time do you bro. Spend time up in that law library; learn the correctional law and the criminal law. Read constantly, stay busy and time will fly.

It's not easy for me to say: been there done that. When I got out of prison I went to John J. College of Criminal Justice. I had gotten my G.E.D., I had plumbing skills and I knew how to read law books. It has never been easy for me, I look back at my past and I regret it and sometimes I don't regret it because these times behind bar had made me a better person. A man of God, a good daddy, a good businessman; from a convict to a C.E.O. and not one company but two companies.

"If any of you lacks wisdom, he should ask God, who gives generously to all without finding fault, and it will be given to him. But when he asks, he must believe and not doubt, because he who doubts is like a wave of the sea, blow and tossed by the wind."
– *James 1:5, 6*

"We live by faith, not by sight."
– 2 Corinthians 5:7

"Blessed is the man whom God corrects; so do not despise but the discipline of the Almighty. For he wounds, but he also binds up; he injures but his hands also heal."
– *Job 5:17, 18*

"Because the Lord disciplines those he loves, and he punishes everyone he accepts as a son."
- Hebrews 12:6

"For what shall it profit a man, if he shall gain the whole world, and he lose his own soul? Or what shall a man give in exchange for his soul?"

- *Mark 8:36,37*

An eternity without God and the good things He has prepared is a terrible price to pay for having our own way over things that will soon pass away. "Seek ye first the kingdom of God, and his righteousness; and all these things shall be added unto you."

I find myself out of the penitentiary with headaches, with tribulations, with a test everyday out in society. Here I am purchasing a new home for investment purposes. Now I'm told that the stainless steel appliances are extra, the ones included in the house are all white and not stainless steel.

I had to run to Mutual Omaha and deposit a check for the amount of $8,400 for a two family house including two dishwashers at $600 dollars each, two refrigerators for $1,500 two microwaves for $400, two stoves for $1,500. I was angry but the builder told me if we wanted Stainless Steel it was extra, it was going to be more than $8,000 plus tax.

I did what any other businessperson would do, take it as a loss and go on. I lost more in the penitentiary, that's my testimony.

I spent many hours in a cell, 23 hours in 1 hour out for recreation – that's how it was each and every day of my life. I think I paid my dues to society and God been good to me.

I took a moment to pray. If you've been where I've been, you'll always take the time to give thanks to the Lord.

"Saying, Amen: Blessing, and glory, and wisdom and thanksgiving, and honour, and power, and might, be unto our God for ever and ever. Amen." – Revalation 7:12

I'm on a new program every day. I'm making my business grow and I cannot do with God's help. There are too many haters out there and no participators. They know so much that they're living with their mother and demand respect. I'm not giving any respect to no momma's boy. It's time to grow up, get out of that cell, do well in parole and get back into college. Get yourself a degree and get yourself a real-estate license. Stop selling drugs and doing wrong, and get your real estate license, and sell state homes.

Here I am listening to my own testimony, I don't ever want to forget the time I spent in Sing- Sing prison, Elmira prison, Collin's correctional facility, Riker's island, the Tombs, the blocks, downstate Correctional facility reception center. It's good to look back at the past and know all the suffering you have gone through like doing time in prison.

I just got the keys for the house, I did the closing for the house – NEXT!

NEXT PROJECT – I'm on the move. I want to keep myself busy and occupied; I have a 9-year-old little girl that needs college money. I don't live for myself, I wake up every morning thanking God and striving like I was cracked out of my mind and I was hustling harder. The entire negative into the positive. It doesn't mean you can't go into the hood and say what's up.

You see me working, it's 10:30 in the morning on top of my game, doing the demos with Wonder Product all-purpose cleaner. Yes I did sell, I don't take no for an answer, my product works, there's no sales pitch here. If it works, they buy. All I do is spray the bottle and if it moves the grease, then it works.

How many cases do you want? I usually work till about 1 o'clock in the afternoon, seven days a week. That's how you progress.

I would always walked around with my laminated newspaper article about my life story, about how I shot somebody in the face for messing with me. Sometimes when you're working, people misjudge you. When they see you on your knees working hard, greasy, they talk shit to you. As a salesman, sometimes people disrespect you. They'll throw you out of their offices and threaten to call the cops for soliciting, and all I'm doing is working under my LLC Corporation.

But I'm sure if I were selling cocaine they would all want some. ☺

I just want you to buy a bottle from me at 12 dollars. 12 times a million is 12 million. I don't need to sell drugs; I'm okay with that. I don't have to be an NFL player or baseball player; I could do all of that in selling homes and manufacturing cleaning products. God has given me a good gift.

I said to myself one day, all of these years have gone by and I said why haven't I thought about this before? Buying homes, building homes, flipping homes instead of selling drugs to my brothers and sisters out there. I got involved buying homes and flipping homes about 10 years ago, I was introduced into the game by an O.G. that also spent many years in the penitentiary. He shared his love with me. So I started my construction company, Lozada Construction LLC.

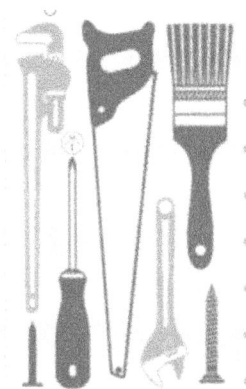

This ain't no drug spot.

WORDS OF GUIDANCE...

"Enter not into the path of the wicked, and go not in the way of evil men." – Proverbs 4:14

Don't ask for trouble by placing yourself in the path of the evildoer. Those are HATERS. We are in the world, but we don't have to be of it. Follow God's way as he says, "This is the way, walk ye in it."

You buy the land, you build on the land.

You bring in the big toys

When times get tough in your life, get yourself a John Deere and dig holes.

Serious toys. When I was being raised in the hood nobody taught me this way of life...

My testimonial, everything is possible through God.

Make a wish come true...

Prayers come true, when you're faithful to God. Don't talk about it, be about it.

This year I've been really kicking ass working hard. But I've got time for my little girl's room. I could've paid somebody to do it for $400, but there's no fun in that. My daughter had asked me to do it.

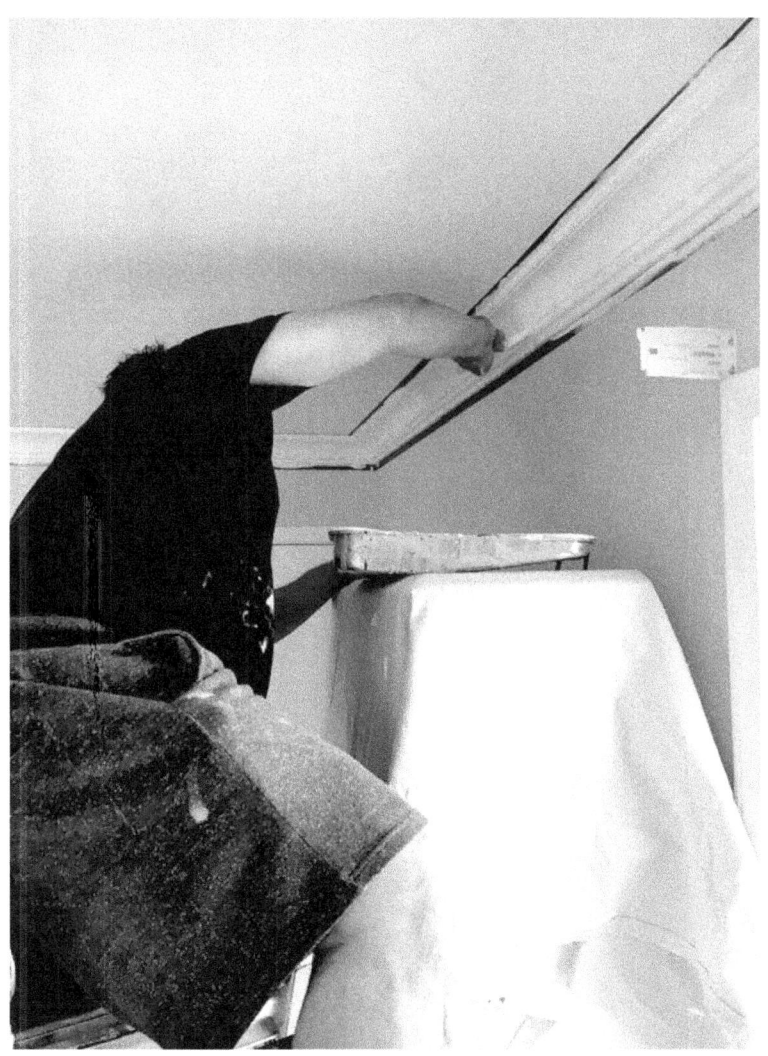

I'm 59 years old, but here I am painting my little girl's room. This is a dream come true, and the Lord knows I am grateful and I talk like that because I want the world to know what God has done for me. Not only did he take me out of prison, opening that cell door but he gave me wisdom, understanding and patience.

I get a satisfaction and I get so sad sometimes that I cry like a little boy, especially when I look into my little girl's eyes and see her face... I always ask "Whatcha want honey?!" ☺

Peer Pressure

I learned this in a prison cell. Fifteen hours away from New York, no mail, no commissary, no visitations solo like bolo. But I had the Bible, I had my street knowledge mi escuelite la calles de Puerto Rico, my survival in the streets of Spanish Harlem. That was in my survival kit. This should also be in your survival kit, my story, my documentary, my time in prison.

"Therefore, I urge you brothers, in view of God's mercy, to offer your bodies as living sacrifices, holy and pleasing to God – this is your spiritual act of worship. Do not conform any longer to the pattern of this world, but be transformed by the renewing of your mind. Then you will be able to test and approve what God's will is – his good, pleasing and perfect will." – Romans 12:1, 2 (NIV)

Don't hate the player, hate the game.

Pride

"For all that is in the world, the lust of the flesh, and the lust of the eyes, and the pride of life, is not of the Father, but is of the world." – 1 John 2:16

Pimping a'int easy.

"LORD, I have heard of your fame; I stand in awe of your deeds, O LORD." Habakkuk 3:2 (NIV)

BORN AGAIN

"For God so loved the world, that he gave his only begotten Son, that whosoever believeth in him should not perish, but have everlasting life." – John 3:16

I should have been in there 59 years ago right in that casket. My little brother was not that fortunate; he got shot in the head on 112th Street and Lexington Avenue, Spanish Harlem. The ones that shot him they're also dead. There are no winners on the streets, la calle. Don't act like you're rough or a killer because you've got 40 tattoos all over your body in some mickey mouse tattoo parlor in the basement. Most of the killers I know in Sing Sing they're doing life and don't have a single tattoo on their body.

But here you are running up and down Washington Heights, Spanish Harlem like you've been in the Attica Riots in Attica Prison. You walk around with your neck all bent up, trying to scare people. You better seek God, swiftly and in a hurry. Nobody cares about you, they're so smoked out they'll shoot your mother and ask questions later. It's a dirty world. Why can't you go to college bro, and get a B.A.? Be a doctor?

Being a wannabe baller or shot-caller and all you're looking for is a thousand years in the penitentiary, but you won't know until you get there my brother.

You're going to be just like this guy who wants to jump off the roof because nobody loves me, because I smoke too much crack, because I was doing heroin, smoking rulers (coke and weed together), and you just have to hit the pipe. Now you find yourself on the roof facing life in prison because you were in the wrong place at the wrong time. There's no second chance here, there's no revolving door with life.

Instead of selling drugs why can't you sell pops? This customer of mine has ten trucks on the streets, he sells a thousand a day and makes 10 thousand at the end of the day. He doesn't have to worry about the DEA, CIA, FBI, ICE, Narcotics Squad, and Robbery Squad... I wish I would've known what I know now. I would have never done 14 years in prison. But with God EVERYTHING is possible, Amen.

I sell this account 5 boxes a year at $144 a case with 12, 32-ounce of fully concentrated cleaner for a total of $720 a year. If I sell $720 a year to a million people a year its seven hundred twenty million. I think that's good enough for me; I don't have to sell drugs. I haven't sold drugs since 1975. Ever since I came out of prison I went straight like an arrow.

The Lord has been good to me so I can flip on him. I just want some toys and pay my daughters college. I'm 59 and she's 10, I want to spend the rest of my life with her. There ain't nothing like being in the penitentiary with kids, its sad so think about it. Watch the movie 'Blow', real sad movie when I saw it I cried like a boy thinking about not waking up with my little girl.

I want to put a smile on my little girl's face.

I want to be the best daddy in the world.

I told my little girl this day to stand ender for a picture

I TRICKED HER. I always do things like that to her.

Look at the smile on my girl's face, she can't believe I did that to her. This is the reason for me to live happily ever after.

I told one of my partners to wash her off now…

I love my toys

Waiting for my daughter to dry up and go home, I need to go into the city later tonight with another toy.

My girl is waiting for the best daddy in the world

WORK HARD, PLAY HARD

Today is Sunday morning; time to be thankful for what God has done for me and especially for my little girl. She motivates my life, keeps me in check and makes me pimp up my life in a new direction. I don't ever want to forget what the Lord has done for me. I'm not trying to brag, I'm just trying to let you know my testament. Since I got out of prison, it's a lesson to be learned for all the wannabe's. The only things out there on the streets are prisons, and more prisons. It's become a corporate enterprise, the prison system. Always waiting for a Spanish fly to get out of line to send him to fly all the way to Elmira prison with 5-10 or 25 to life. It's your pick.

Why try to get your life together and get college credits in prison when you can do it on the streets at Hunter College, John Jay College of Criminal law and criminal justice. Why not be a professor, an attorney, a doctor or engineer? Instead of being on the streets looking for time to be served at a penitentiary. I wish I had known better, yet I had to spend all that time in a cell wasting my time trying to get a G.E.D. and college credits to look good in front of a parole board. I should have done my time on the streets, that's why today I'm writing my life story. Maybe, I could get through your hard head a little bit and keep you on the streets instead of the penitentiary. For those that are in the penitentiary, do your 5's, 10's, 15's and on learning something in there, seeking God faithfully like I did – the Lord's been good to me.

HOW TO BE BORN AGAIN:

"That which is born of the flesh is flesh; and that which is born of the Spirit is spirit." – John 3:6

"But God, who is rich in mercy, for his great love wherewith he loved us, Even when we were dead in sins, hath quickened us together with Christ... For by grace are ye saved through faith; and that not of yourselves: it is the gift of God: not of works, lest any man should boast." – Ephesians 2:4,5,8,9

"For all have sinned, and come short of the glory of God." – Romans 3:23

That same morning I got up and told my girl to get my dog and check on our crops in the backyard, I'm trying to stay organic. I also learned that in the penitentiary when I was working at C-Block in Elmira in the mess hall. From 3:30 in the morning until breakfast was over.

My daughter and my pure breed brindle blue nose pit-bull. I got him for my little girl on her birthday, he's her protector.

I always take my dog for a walk, always looking around for the foxes

When my daughter was born, I always told God that I would make my daughter go to church on Sundays so that the blessings may keep coming.

"Love is patient, love is king. It does not envy, it does not boast, it is not proud. It is not rude, it is not self –seeking, it is not easily angered, and it keeps no record of wrongs. Love does not delight in evil but rejoices with the truth. It always protects, always trusts, always hopes, always perseveres…Love never fails." – 1 Corinthians 13:4-8 (NIV)

CHAPTER 15
2016

I took my daughter to the Health & Fitness Expo at Metlife Stadium and took pictures with the New Jersey state troopers. My daughter was so excited.

Gracias Veronica por todo y los vemos pronto en una de las peleas in Madison Square Garden or Barclay Center ☺

My daughter with Veronica Contreras from Channel 47 Telemundo Sports.

Thank you for always showing me love in the sports world

My girl having a blast

J.T. Thomas, he signed a three year contract for a cool $12 million with the New York Giants, here he is with my daughter and me. You don't see him doing time in the

penitentiary, a true testimony right here. You don't have to sell drugs or do any crime to come up, ALL THE WAY UP, like Fat Joe says.

I'm having a great day, and I owe all of this to the one up there that took me out of a prison cell and gave me wisdom, understanding, patience and appreciation for freedom & life.

When I met George, I told him my name is George too – they call me Jorge Lozada or Georgie, or Jorgito. He smiled at me and I said "It's a pleasure meeting you, I've seen your show before" and I asked him questions about construction, he didn't hold back. He was honest and gave me some good tips. Today, I am the C.E.O. of Lozada Construction, LLC. It's not who you are, it's who you know. Ask questions for you to know what to do in life, besides selling drugs out in the hood and ending up at Riker's then being shipped out to Attica, Greenhaven, Elmira Gladiator school of boxing. Learn a trade instead, do you.

In my career of the penitentiary, I met a lot of guys say they're going to do and never do anything. When they find themselves in the penitentiary with 1,000 years the wake up call is too late in the game. Checkmate. I've been there, many nights, my birthday, my brother's death, my aunt passing away and family members one by one. There's always a second chance, regardless if you've done 5, 10 or 15 years or you're on the street lost. If you're on the street you've got the upper hand now partner, pimp up. Criminology 101, Pimpinology 101.

From Jorge Lozada to David Ushery: You're the man.

My boy Jorge Ramos & the whole cast of Noticiero Telemundo Channel 47
Gracias Jorge Ramos, for your mad love. Every time you see me you give me lots of love, gracias ☺

To Rob Shmitt, the player: Always looking good ☺

I'm just having fun trying to be a judge, but I do have the experience to be a judge. I know what a good performance is, I did Apollo Theater with my salsa band many years ago. I got first place for a Latin salsa band.

This is me in the penitentiary. I used to practice for hours at a time; I did time, time didn't do me. I read law books, I took business courses, I stayed to me. I wasn't in there for any bag of weed, I was there for murder from Spanish Harlem across 110th Street. Frank Luca & Nicky Barnes neighborhood; that's how I got my degree in Criminology 101.

That's how I did my time.

That's the reason why I'm writing this book. To show you the inside and the outside of your life path and career in this world. That's pimpinology, you better get it now while you're on the streets. Seek God first and all things will be given to you. When I got out of the penitentiary, I was standing on 42nd street with a bus ticket and a voucher for the shelter. I was tired of doing time, of being stupid and ignorant. That's my true story. I've cried many, many nights feeling sorry for myself. It was nothing easy doing that time, 23 in and 1 hour for recreation only. Until I woke up one day and smelled the coffee, I wanted to turn my life around.

Especially now that I have my daughter, all bets are off now. I'm really going to pimp up and travel with my daughter, get her the best education and make her happy. Give her the things I've never had. It isn't about me anymore, God's been good to me.

I worked this year so hard, but I shouldn't complain because I used to mop the floors of the penitentiary for a dollar a day. I decided to take my wife for a vacation, my daughter and some friends of mine. That's how it is each and every day of my life, thankful and grateful.

Check in time with the wolf pack at Great Wolf Lodge.

It's 1 a.m. and my girl and I are still hanging out.

In her wolf den bunk bed

Enjoying herself, so she can do well in school. That's the deal I made with her ☺

Enjoying the morning buffet; I always get flashbacks when I eat good food now, it reminds me of days I was in a cell hungry.

Starbucks and the wolf, what else can I ask for? Life is good.

Making my daughter happy

Hanging with the wolves

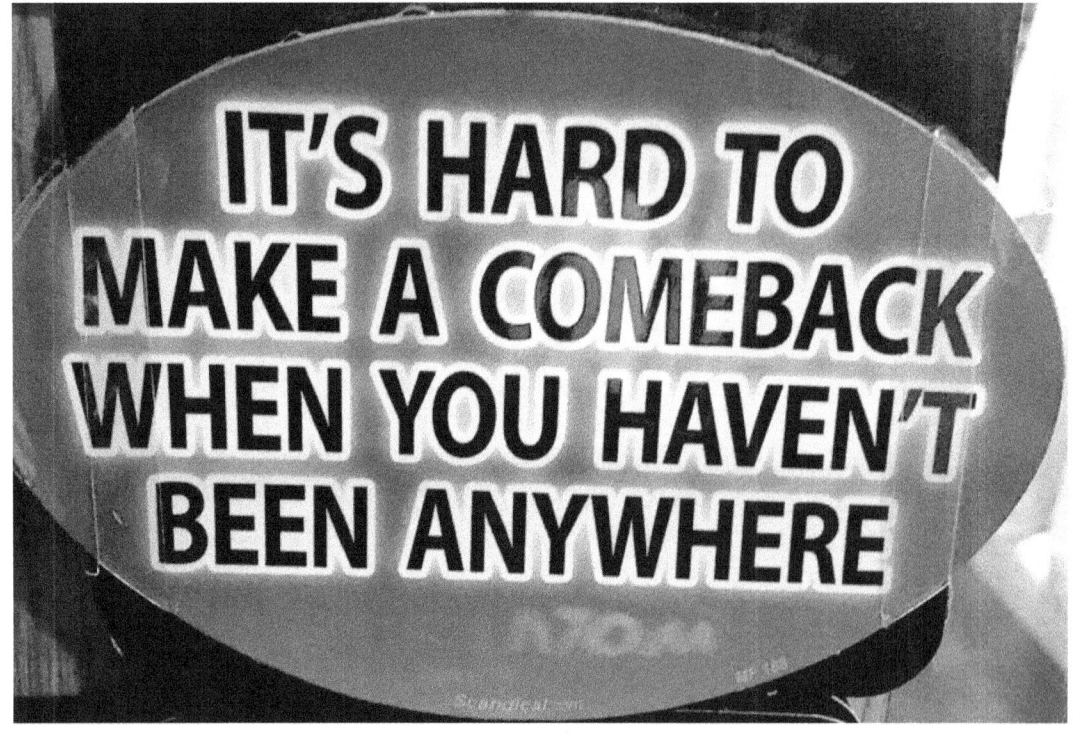

True story.

My life, my wife, and my daughter. Thank you God, you're so good to me. Thank you for my freedom.

True story.

You've got to keep the wolf around at all times

Don't get it twisted, partner.

I used to hang out with all the inmates at the penitentiary but now I hang out with the wolves.

What a beautiful day

Find my daughter and I on the Boat

Mother and daughter having a good time

Second day and I'm tired, but my daughter has me going at 9 a.m. to the pool

Chasing my daughter around the store, I'm 59 and I need to enjoy every minute I have with my daughter.

The champ is tired after a long day of activities

On the third day my daughter wanted to participate in a obstacle course...

Here she is finishing the course

On the last day my General manager and his wife came to visit us and spend the day

Time to check out but they don't want to check out ☺

I told her we were going to another trip again, she believes me. I keep all my promises with her.

I sit here in my office, and I feel so blessed that I don't want to speak just Christian to you especially if you're inside a cell. You're in a cell for 20 years, I say to you: "Start writing a book from the penitentiary. We need brothers like you that have been through hell and back, or are in hell. We need your love, your experience, especially when you're doing time because most of the time when you're in the box with 23 hours in and 1 hour for recreation, I know the feeling – I've been there. You speak from the heart especially when you spend that time for so long in a cell, months, years, hours and tears."

Write! Let the brothers know, your experiences and what you're going through. What it is to be in PRISON. It is no joke, and at the same time you make money with the books. You might get a movie deal… Don't waste your time bro, getting more time inside the penitentiary. Spend a lot of time in that law library, like you want to get out. Start taking courses inside the penitentiary, get college credits and get a degree. Prepare yourself for the world!

When I first got out, I stayed in a shelter. I stayed on the streets and had no direction in my life. Through the years, of being 'en la calle y el baja mundo', I've met hundreds of people that wanted to help me because the type of person I was. I kept it real, but at the end of the day I always turn to God. I didn't waste my time in the penitentiary, got my GED, took college courses; I took a legal research course to become a jailhouse lawyer and law clerk. I helped hundreds of Boricuas that couldn't speak English from Riker's all the way to Elmira prison, helping them with their legal work and translating what charges they had. I'm in the law books officially.

Don't think, no te creas that I didn't have conflicts with other lifers. For some reason or another, I moved so fast that I had haters in the penitentiary too. They knew about me, I stayed most of the time by myself in the law library trying my best to get out of penitentiary. When it came to the dominos, the basketball court, gambling and the drug & gangs scene I stayed to myself just like I did on the streets. It wasn't easy but I'm here and you can be here too. TRUE DOCUMENTARY.

You want to come up; all the way up you don't have to do it my way, do you because I'm not going to do the rest of your time. All I want to give is show you love; show you a way out of prison. Avoid the things that God hates, my brother.

I write them down, you read them and you make your choice in the penitentiary or on the streets with your daughter, your son, or your family. I choose to be with my daughter, I choose to be free.

"There are six things the Lord hates, seven that are detestable to him: haughty eyes, a lying tongue, hands that shed innocent blood, a heart that devises wicked schemes, feet that are quick to rush into evil, a false witness who pours out lies, and a man who stirs up dissension among brothers" – Proverbs 6:16-19, NIV

I forgot to tell you, I spent a lot of time listening to Willie Rosario's 'Botaron La Pelota', Andy Montanes, El Grand Combo de Puerto Rico, Marvin Santiago, Hector Lavoe my personal friend and Camacho's friend, Ray Barretto, Pete Elconde. Listening to Salsa and reading the word kept me afloat, until now.

Labor Day Weekend 2016

Standing here, thanking God for my blessings.

The dog in me ☺

Te estoy belando, I'm watching you ☺

I don't even drink but its all here

I took a selfie

That's what I work for, my daughter, my wife, my friends and God. But I've always got time to talk to the less unfortunate, don't get the poor, the prisoners, you have to be grateful to God for your life, your freedom.

I told you man, not to mess with me but no, you wouldn't listen to me so see you now! You see yourself now. Now you believe me. ☺

Cooking up a storm, Italian Style

See, I told you I could make a pizza ☺

Don't hate the player, hate the game. Don't focus on me, focus on you. Read the bible, go to church, seek God and all things will be manifested to you. I didn't spend 14 years in the penitentiary because I wanted to, and I'm definitely not proud but I'm being a true example for those that come home and don't go back to hell.

NFL Player Evan Rodriguez at one of his spots over Labor Day Weekend 2016. I was invited to his baby shower.

Evan, his beautiful wife Olivia and me

This is a true example of a brother with no father, no mother that could be up in Sing Sing prison, but he decided to go to college, be an NFL player and a businessman.

My daughter and I getting drunk off soda, and all the food Evan had at his baby shower

Thank you for having us Evan, the food & presentation was excellent at your spot.

I'm at a bike show with my daughter and Jason Britton, Ian Gaines – stuntmen for movies.

My daughter collecting the autographs

My girl trying to talk me into buying that bike for her

Don't mess with the little girl, she's got security ☺

Hanging with the toys

Hanging with Moe, District Manager for Kawasaki & Scott, General Manager for Sales at Extreme Machine. We're going for a ride, early in the morning. You see my Dunkin Donuts there... ☺

To purchase it's $29.95 with shipping included...

P.O. Box 6196, Monroe Township, N.J. 08831

WONDER : ALL PURPOSE CLEANER

Fully concentrated, citrus based. Send money orders to address listed above.

Moe, I'll always be grateful to you for helping me introduce my cleaner and get some accounts.

Going out for a ride at 7 a.m. to the track

The next day, going to the woods to go mudding

Later on in the evening, I'm teaching my daughter some tricks on how to play pool.

She's teaching me how to take a shot

I'm not surprised, she made the shot. I taught her good ☺

"An evil man is trapped by his sinful talk, but a righteous man escapes trouble-" – Proverbs 12:13, NIV

"A fool gets into constant fights. His mouth is his undoing! His words endanger him-" – Proverbs 18:6-7, TLB

I'm preaching at you now.

There's a time and place for everything, I choose to spend the rest of my life with my little girl.

SELF-CONTROL

"But the fruit of the Spirit is love, joy, peace, patience, kindness, goodness, faithfulness, gentleness, and self-control. Against such things there is no law." – Galatians 5:22, 23 (NIV)

COURAGE

"Be strong and courageous, be not afraid nor dismayed or the king of Assyria, nor for all the multitude that is with him: for there be more with us than with him: With him is an arm of flesh; but with us is the LORD our Gold to help us, and to fight our battles…." – 2 Chronicles 32:7, 8

"Anyone willing to be corrected is on the pathway to life. Anyone refusing has lost his chance" – Proverbs 10:17, TLB

I'm not a preacher, but I spent many nights listening to Jose Alberto's 'El Canario', "A La Hora Que Me Llamen Voy" in a cell. My bible would be open, reading through scriptures and using the word to better myself, to be more humble, positive about the future. You see, when you get to prison that's when you have the most time to think about your mistakes, about what went wrong for you to end up there with 25 to life.

You only think about it afterwards.

I would listen to Marc Anthony in my cell at 3:30 in the morning, from my Walkman. "El Cantante" would come on, and tears would stream down from my eyes recalling when I used to live on East 110th Street and share moments with Hector Lavoe. Memories about Hector Camacho would flash in my mind. Many nights I spent in after hours at Gallery on 110th Street between 2nd and 1st on the second floor, sniffing cocaine until the next day. I am grateful that I'm alive.

"I love those who love me, and those who seeks me find me... Blessed is at the man who listens to me, watching daily at my doors, waiting at my doorway" – Proverbs 8:17,34, NIV

"Because the Lord is my Sheperd, I have everything I need!" – Psalm 23:1, TLB

Put God's work first – above all personal needs.

3I ended up in prison not thinking, moving too fast and every time I wound up in prison that's when my brain used to 'click'. For the young brothers out there or incarcerated in New York State prisons or anywhere else in the world, whether its Puerto Rico, Santo Domingo, Colombia, Africa, Haiti, Spanish Harlem, BK, Brooklyn, Jamaica Avenue, Texas, Ft. Lauderdale, Miami, East Coast, West Coast – Go get yourself a college degree, in Business – strive to be a CEO. Before you wind up in a cold ass, damp cell for years. True story. This is the Game, I'm pimping at you. I'm telling you my story, and while I sit here writing this book I shed tears.

Sometimes, we're just hardheaded. We like it hard and rough. I promise you, if you read the Bible and follow the word of God and be a GANGSTER for GOD you will succeed in life. They thought I was crazy, when I would read the word in my cell while they played Basketball and every time my cell opened up; faith in my prayers has been answered. I've seen miracles, but you'd probably think I'm crazy that I'm saying this but now he's become a preacher, he's a man of God. I'm just a believer.

Acquire blessings and wealth only according to God's plan.

I am so grateful to God that I got a second chance

Yo soy de aqui como el coqui

I am listening to old school music from Willie Rosario, la "luvia" is playing and thinking about being incarcerated, I get flashbacks all the time. Flashbacks about the food I used to eat, the mail, the visits, everything a man could only experience while he's in a cell 23 hours a day, 1 hour out.

All these things are material, cars, houses, credit cards, mortgages, taxes – but life itself is a challenge, problems everyday. Road rage on the streets of New York everyday, it feels like I'm in prison again not knowing when someone is going to go off. That's the reason these days that I seek God because its impossible for me to deal with society especially when you first come home from prison after doing 14 years. It's tough. So whom do you turn to?

GOD.

It worked for me.

MY DOCUMENTARY.

"Work hard and become a leader; be lazy and never succeed" – Proverbs 12:24, TLB

"Because the Lord disciplines those he loves, as a father the son he delights in." – Proverbs 3:12

"Blessed is the man whom God corrects; so do not despise the discipline of the Almighty. For he wounds, but he also binds up; he injures, but his hands also heal." – Job 5:17,18

I was once in the yard on a parole violation in Sing Sing prison in Ossining, New York. I met an old timer there that had been down 22 years and had about 30 years to go and he said, "I was just like you, in and out of prison for years until one day I went along on an armed robbery with a couple of guys. It was supposed to be a quick job, in and out. They forgot the main element of the movie, and that's when anything can go wrong in a robbery. Someone got killed. And I wound up with 52 to life, and I didn't even squeeze the trigger. I was just the chauffer."

When I heard him telling me his true DOCUMENTARY he looked at my eyes with tears dripping down his face he said, "Seek God bro, you're young, don't be like me. No one cares from the outside world when you're here, not your brother, not your sister, not your friends. Maybe your mother will come up, if she's still alive."

TRUE STORY.

It gets very cold in the winter, crime doesn't pay.

It gets very lonely here, crime doesn't pay.

Ask someone that has been here 20 years, crime doesn't pay.

If you wish to give your family up for this, crime doesn't pay.

Your mother might die while you're incarcerated, crime doesn't pay.

You won't see your little girl grow up, crime doesn't pay.

You will hear that auntie passed away, uncle passed away, crime doesn't pay.

OR I GUARANTEE, This will be your new home. Christmas, New Years, Thanksgiving, Halloween, Your Birthday, Mom's Birthday, Daughter's Graduation, Father's Funeral, Grandma's Wake.

THE PROMISE

"I tell you the truth, he who believes has everlasting life." – John 6:47

"Then Jesus declared, "I am the bread of life. He who comes to me will never go hungry, and he who believes in me will never be thirsty." – John 6:35

Very cold in those cells, crime really doesn't pay.

Very hot during the summer, inmates are dying, crime doesn't pay.

When I got out for that hour of recreation, I would play my trombone for that whole hour. I would do all my exercises in my cell. I've been there.

Everything you do on the street, this is where you pay for it.

BAJA MUNDO

Just graduated from the streets, here's your limo to your graduation.

After graduation, the club door is open all for you. Guaranteed you wont like it, just think about it for a minute and meditate. If you're already there, and you're reading my story, my documentary, you know what time it is. I am sure you read the word of God at night. Pull your pants up, crime don't pay.

If I would have known what I know now, I would have never, and I mean never ever would I have done the things that I regret in my life today. I didn't know any better, no father, no mother but that's not an excuse. I won't sit here and give you excuses. I had opportunities; I just didn't have a father figure. If I had known that a college degree could be accomplished in 5-6 years instead of 14 years in prison with a record, I would have taken a different road. I just didn't know any better.

I'm not Lucky Luciano, I'm J. Lozada that grew up in the hood and ate & slept in the hood. So what do I get? The hood.

You, you've got a shot at the world. Now that you've read my documentary, and you've seen the pictures of my life story, you've been warned and you've been told:

WHAT TIME IT IS

"Whether you turn to the right or to the left, your ears will hear a voice behind you, saying, "This is the way; walk in It." – Isaiah 30:21

"For this God is our God for ever and ever; he will be our guide even to the end." – Psalms 48:14

I will lead the blind by ways they have not known, along unfamiliar paths I will guide them; I will turn the darkness into light before them and make the rough places smooth. These are the things I will do; I will not forsake them." – Isaiah 42:16

"The righteousness of the blameless makes a straight way for them, but the wicked are brought down by their own wickedness." – Proverbs 11:5

"I will instruct you and teach you in the way you should go; I will counsel you and watch over you." – Psalms 32:8

Now you're not pimping backwards.

"You are the God who performs miracles; you display your power among the peoples."
– Psalm 77:14 (NIV)

"But though he had done so many miracles before them, yet they believed not on him..." – John 12:37

"You will have plenty to eat, until you are full, and you will praise the name of the Lord your God, who has worked wonders for you; never again will my people be shamed." – Joel 2:26

"The Lord is my light and my salvation – whom shall I fear? The Lord is the stronghold of my life – of whom shall I be afraid? ... Though an army besiege me, my heart will not fear; though war break out against me, even then will I be confident." – Psalms 27:1, 3

I decided to write this documentary to give a piece of mind to my brothers doing hard time in prison. Attica, Sing Sing, Collins 1, Collins 2, Riker's Island, Downstate Correctional, Danamora, State of Florida, Puerto Rico prisons – there's hope outside of those walls. I'm not asking you to be a preacher or a fanatic to the Christian world, walking around the prison with a bible faking the move to keep the dogs off you. To manipulate the system and make them believe you're a changed man; it doesn't work that way, God knows your heart. I spent many hours on my knees, seeking faithfully and I'm not ashamed.

I was in a cell, on my knees faithfully asking God to change my heart, my ways. To make me a pimp for him, make me a gangster for him. It's not easy being Christian, people judge you for your actions, and they hate you for your possessions. But I was the one in that cell doing that time, and I know what the Lord has done for me. I am just telling you my story.

"O Lord my God, in thee do I put my trust: save me from all them that persecute me, and deliver me." – Psalm 7:1

"If you belong to the Lord, reverence him; for everyone who does this has everything he needs" – Psalm 34;9, TLB

"What I want from you is your true thanks; I want your promises fulfilled. I want you to trust me in your times of trouble, so I can rescue you, and you can give me your glory" – Psalm 50:14-15, TLB

TRUST GOD FOR ALL THINGS

I took the day off to meet a man that has been an inspiration in my life. I went to go meet with him at the golf course and get some advice. He's a man of God and very successful in life, owning about 10 hotel properties and never smoked a joint in his life or did drugs. He started from scratch by himself. True story.

I love my freedom, I would hate to be incarcerated.

"...How shall we escape if we ignore such a great salvation? This salvation, which was first announced by the Lord, was confirmed to us by those who heard him. God also testified to it by signs, wonders, and various miracles, and gifts of the Holy Spirit distributed according to His will." – Hebrews 2:3,4 (NIV)

CHAPTER 16

Most of the time, we don't think, we act and sometimes when we wake up from that dream and we sober up, reality sets in then you have a half a million-dollar bail and no one to help you. Reality sets in. I'm saying this from experience, I would hear men late in the morning on their knees asking the Lord for forgiveness when they have 25 to life, crying out to God. I've seen a lot of gangsters on their knees, and hard-core killers turn their life around to God. I must be making the right decision to seek the Lord. These are guys that have been down 20 years and they're never, ever getting out from behind the walls, the loneliest place that nobody remembers you. It's easy to forget about you while you're in there.

No one cares about you, and this is just Riker's Island. There's no such thing as protective custody. They want you, they're going to get you especially if you harmed a kid, an elderly or mother. You're going to get it.

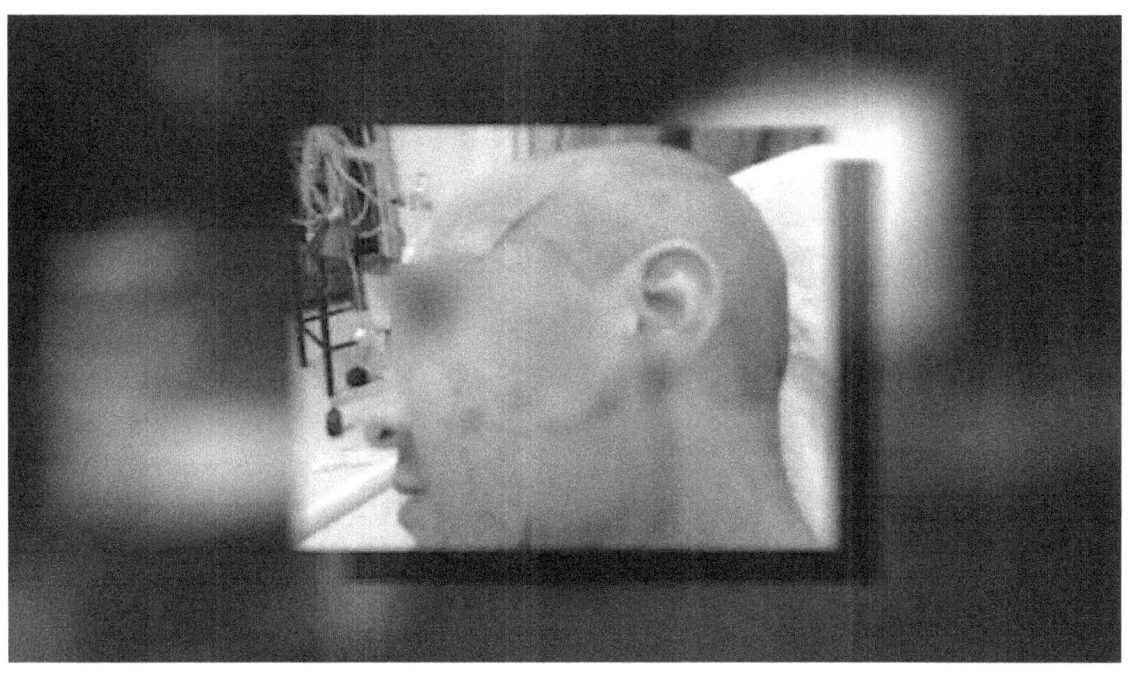

"Put on the whole armour of God, that ye may be able to stand against the wiles of the devil." – Ephesians 6:11

"But if our gospel be hid, it is hid to them that are lost: In whom the god of this world hath blinded the minds of them which believe not, lest the light of the glorious gospel of Christ, who is the image of God, should shine unto them." – 2 Corinthians 4:3, 4

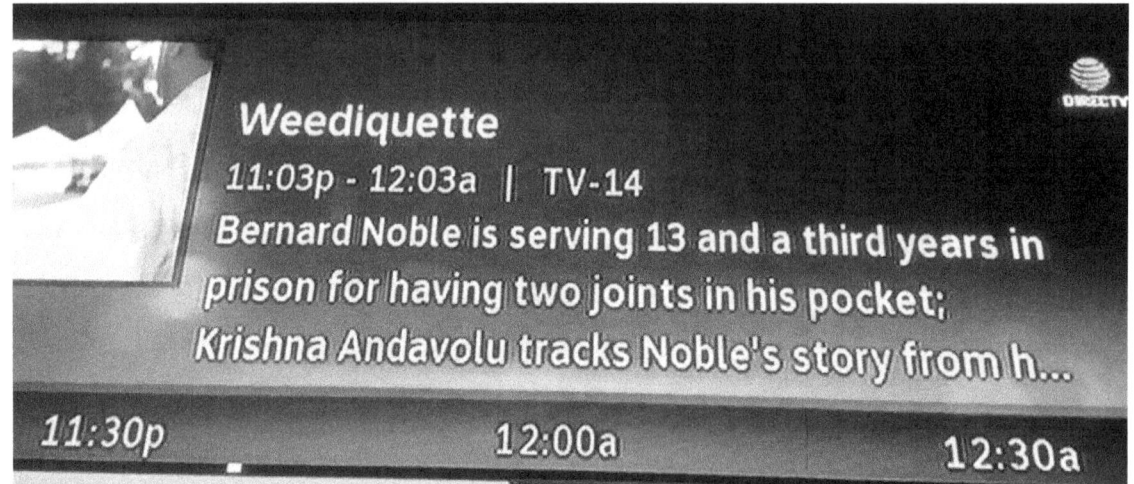

You see, what happens in cases like this is that we as a kid build a criminal record of petty crimes and plea bargain to a felony. When you get three of those, you're in for life. The first time you get mad at someone and you hit them with a bat, or you rob a car. Anything petty that carries a felony, you're going away for life. True story.

Going back to the future, I choose this prison cell and I choose God over the penitentiary.

FAME

"Lord, I have heard of your fame; I stand in awe of your deeds, O LORD." – Habakkuk 3:2 (NIV)

"Therefore, I urge you, brothers, in view of God's mercy, to offer your bodies as living sacrifices,, holy and pleasing to God-this is your spiritual act of worship. Do not conform any longer to the pattern of this world, but be transformed by the renewing of your mind. Then you will be able to test and approve what God's will is – his good, pleasing and perfect will." – Romans 12:1, 2 (NIV)

"What I want from you is your true thanks; I want your promises fulfilled. I want you to trust me in your times of trouble, so I can rescue you, and you can give me glory." – Psalm 50:14-15, TLB

"Every word of God proves true. He defends all who come to him for protection." – Proverbs 30:5, TLB

<u>Seek God's counsel before acting on any matter.</u>

"Without wise leadership, a nation is in trouble; but with good counselors there is safety." – Proverbs 11:14, TLB

"A fool thinks he needs no advice, but a wise man listens to others." – Proverbs 12:15, TLB

"A man who refuses to admit his mistakes can never be successful. But if he confesses and forsakes them, he gets another CHANCE." – Proverbs 28:13, TLB

True story

www.ingramcontent.com/pod-product-compliance
Lightning Source LLC
Chambersburg PA
CBHW080724230426
43665CB00020B/2611